Marian Cox

Measure for Measure

William Shakespeare

Philip Allan Updates
Market Place
Deddington
Oxfordshire
OX15 0SE
Tel: 01869 338652
Fax: 01869 337590
e-mail: sales@philipallan.co.uk
www.philipallan.co.uk

© Philip Allan Updates 2005

ISBN-13 978-1-84489-216-7
ISBN-10 1-84489-216-6

In all cases we have attempted to trace and credit copyright owners of material used.

Printed by MPG Books, Bodmin

Environmental information
The paper on which this title is printed is sourced from mills using wood from managed, sustainable forests.

P00499

Contents

Introduction

Aims of the guide

The purpose of this Student Text Guide to *Measure for Measure* is to enable you to organise your thoughts and responses to the play, to deepen your understanding of key features and aspects, and finally to help you to address the particular requirements of examination questions in order to obtain the best possible grade. It will also prove useful to those of you writing a coursework piece on the play by providing summaries, lists, analyses and references to help with the content and construction of the assignment. Line references in this guide refer to the *New Penguin Shakespeare* edition of the play.

It is assumed that you have read and studied the play already under the guidance of a teacher. This Student Text Guide is a revision guide, not an introduction, although some of its content serves the purpose of providing initial background. It can be read in its entirety in one sitting, or it can be dipped into and used as a reference guide to specific and separate aspects of the play.

The remainder of this *Introduction* consists of exam board specifications and Assessment Objectives and a revision scheme which gives a suggested programme for using the material in the guide. A section on writing examination essays gives extensive practical advice on writing essay answers.

The *Text Guidance* section consists of a series of subsections which examine key aspects of the play including contexts, scene summaries, themes and imagery. Emboldened terms within the Text Guidance section are glossed in 'Literary terms and concepts' on pp. 81–84.

The final section, *Questions and Answers*, gives examples of essay questions of different types, and includes exemplar essay plans and samples of marked work.

Exam board specifications

Measure for Measure is currently a set text on two exam boards and three specifications, all at A2.

OCR	A2 Unit 2710	Closed book	Edition not specified
AQA Spec A	A2 Unit 4	Closed book	Edition not specified
AQA Spec B	A2 Unit 5	Closed book	Edition not specified

Assessment Objectives

The Assessment Objectives for A-level English Literature are common to all boards:

AO1	communicate clearly the knowledge, understanding and insight appropriate to literary study, using appropriate terminology and accurate and coherent written expression
AO2i	respond with knowledge and understanding to literary texts of different types and periods
AO2ii	respond with knowledge and understanding to literary texts of different types and periods, exploring and commenting on relationships and comparisons between literary texts
AO3	show detailed understanding of the ways in which writers' choices of form, structure and language shape meanings
AO4	articulate independent opinions and judgements, informed by different interpretations of literary texts by other readers
AO5i	show understanding of the contexts in which literary texts are written and understood
AO5ii	evaluate the significance of cultural, historical and other contextual influences on literary texts and study

A summary and paraphrase of each Assessment Objective is given below and would be worth memorising:

AO1	clarity of written communication
AO2	informed personal response in relation to time and genre (literary context)
AO3	the creative literary process (context of writing)
AO4	critical and interpretative response (context of reading)
AO5	evaluation of influences (cultural context)

Measure for Measure has a total weighting of 30%, divided as follows:

OCR	AO1 – 5%; AO2ii – 5%; AO3 – 5%; AO4 – 10%; AO5ii – 5%
AQA Spec A	AO1 – 6%; AO2ii – 5%; AO3 – 6%; AO4 – 13%
AQA Spec B	AO1 – 10%; AO5ii – 20%

Note the different weighting of Assessment Objectives between the different examining boards for the same text. It is essential that you pay close attention to the AOs, and their weighting, for the board for which you are entered. These are what the examiner will be looking for, and you must address them *directly* and *specifically*, in addition to proving general familiarity with and understanding of the text, and being able to present an argument clearly, relevantly and convincingly.

Remember that the examiners are seeking above all else evidence of an informed personal response to the text. A revision guide such as this can help you to understand the text and to form your own opinions, and can suggest areas to think about it, but it cannot replace your own ideas and responses as an individual reader.

Revision advice

For the examined units it is possible that either brief or extensive revision will be necessary because the original study of the text took place some time previously. It is therefore as well to know how to go about revising and which tried and tested methods are considered the most successful for literature exams at all levels, from GCSE to degree finals.

Below is a guide on how not to do it. Think of reasons why not in each case. **Don't**:
- leave it until the last minute
- assume that revision is unnecessary because you remember the text well
- spend hours designing a beautiful revision schedule
- revise more than one text at the same time
- decide in advance what you think the questions will be and revise only for those
- try to memorise particular essay plans
- reread texts randomly and aimlessly
- revise for longer than two hours in one sitting
- miss school lessons in order to work alone at home
- try to learn a whole ring-binder's worth of work
- tell yourself that character and plot revision is enough
- imagine that watching the video again is the best way to revise
- rely on a study guide instead of the text

There are no short-cuts to effective exam revision; the only one way to know a text extremely well, and to know your way around it in an exam, is to have done the necessary studying. If you use the following method, in six easy stages, you will not only revisit and reassess all previous work on the text but be able to distil, organise and retain your knowledge.

(1) Between a month and a fortnight before the exam, depending on your schedule (a simple list of stages with dates to display in your room, not a work of art!), you will need to reread the text, this time taking stock of all the underlinings and marginal annotations as well. As you read, collect onto sheets of A4 the essential ideas and quotations as you come across them. The acts of selecting key material and recording it as notes are natural ways of stimulating thought and aiding memory.

(2) Reread the highlighted areas and marginal annotations in your critical extracts and background handouts, and add anything useful from them to your list of notes and quotations. Then reread your previous essays and the teacher's comments. As you look back through essays written earlier in the course you should have the pleasant sensation of realising that you can now write much better on the text than you could then. You will also discover that much of your huge file of notes is redundant or repeated, and that you have changed your mind about some beliefs, so that the distillation process is not too daunting. Selecting what is important is the way to crystallise your knowledge and understanding.

(3) During the run-up to the exam you need to do lots of practice essay plans to help you identify any gaps in your knowledge and give you practice in planning in 5–8 minutes. Past paper titles for you to plan from are provided in this guide, some of which can be done as full timed essays, which will show whether length and timing are problematic for you. If you have not seen a copy of a real exam paper before you take your first module, ask to see a past paper so that you are familiar with the layout, rubric and types of question. It would also be helpful if your teacher shared with you the examiners' reports on past papers.

(4) About a week before the exam, reduce your two or three sides of A4 notes to a double-sided postcard of very small, dense writing. Collect a group of key words by once again selecting and condensing, and use abbreviations for quotations (first and last word), character names and place names (initials). Choosing and writing out the short quotations will help you to focus on the essential issues, and to recall them quickly in the exam. Make sure that your selection covers the main themes and includes examples of imagery, language, style, comments on character, examples of irony and other significant aspects of the text. Previous class discussion and essay writing will have indicated which quotations are useful for almost any title; pick those which can serve more than one purpose. In this way a minimum number of quotations can have maximum application.

(5) You now have in a compact, accessible form all the material for any possible essay title. There are only half a dozen themes relevant to a literary text, so if you have covered these you should not meet with any nasty surprises when you read the exam questions. You do not need to refer to your file of paperwork again, or even to the text. For the few days before the exam you can read through your handy postcard

whenever and wherever you get the opportunity. Each time you read it, which will take only a few minutes, you are reminding yourself of all the information you will be able to recall in the exam to adapt to the general title or to support an analysis of particular passages.

(6) A fresh, active mind works wonders, and information needs time to settle, so don't try to cram just before the exam. Relax the night before and get a good night's sleep. Then you will be able to enter the exam room feeling the confidence of the well-prepared but relaxed candidate.

Coursework

It is possible that you are doing *Measure for Measure* as a Shakespeare or other coursework text. If so, you must be sure that your title(s), negotiated with your teacher, fits the Assessment Objectives and their respective weighting for your board. Coursework must be between 1,500 and 2,000 words on all boards. If you are obliged to, or choose to, write two pieces (depending on the board), consideration will need to be given to how the two relate to each other and cover different aspects of the text without overlap.

The coursework writing process differs from an examination in being more leisurely and more supported by the discussion and drafting stages, but the issues of the text remain the same, as does the need for a relevant, focused response to the title. Coursework should be word-processed in the interests of presentation, consideration for the examiner, and ease of alteration for the student.

There are a number of key stages in the coursework writing process:
- Once you have decided on the title and you are familiar with the Assessment Objectives, reread the play and all the notes and annotations you have made, extracting what is relevant for your title.
- With teacher guidance, read some background material and critical essays, and collect relevant information from them. Keep a list of books and articles you have consulted. Rephrase any ideas you borrow from elsewhere.
- Write a one-page essay plan, consisting of subheadings and main points, and show it to your teacher to ensure that you have fully covered the title and have adopted an appropriate essay structure.
- Write a draft of the essay, roughly the right length, based on your plan. Use details, examples and quotations from the text to support your points.
- Read through your draft, making sure that you have fully answered and remained focused on the question. Submit your draft to your teacher in good time.
- When your draft is returned, put into practice the comments offered to help you improve your essay and its grade, and adjust the length if necessary.
- Produce the final version, improving content, expression and accuracy where

possible. Check the final word count. Include a bibliography listing the texts you have quoted from or consulted in your writing of the essay.

■ After a final read through, putting yourself in the position of the reader, make last-minute adjustments and submit your essay — before the deadline.

Writing examination essays

Essay content

One of the key skills you are being asked to demonstrate at A-level is the ability to select and tailor your knowledge of the text and its background to the question set in the exam paper. In order to reach the highest levels, you need to avoid 'pre-packaged' essays which lack focus, relevance and coherence, and which simply contain everything you know about the text. Be ruthless in rejecting irrelevant material, after considering whether it can be made relevant by a change of emphasis. Aim to cover the whole question, not just part of it; your response needs to demonstrate breadth and depth, covering the full range of text elements: character, event, theme and language. Only half a dozen essay approaches are possible for any set text, though they may be phrased in a variety of ways, and they are likely to refer to the key themes of the text. Preparation of the text therefore involves extensive discussion and practice at manipulating these core themes so that there should be no surprises in the exam. An apparently new angle is more likely to be something familiar presented in an unfamiliar way and you should not panic or reject the choice of question because you think you know nothing about it.

Read essay questions twice; the focus is not always immediately obvious. Many of them are several lines long, with several parts or sentences, some of which may be quotations from critics or from the text. You need to be sure of what a title is getting at, and the assumptions behind it, before you decide to reject it or attempt it.

Different views

Exam titles are open-ended in the sense that there is no obvious right answer, and you would therefore be unwise to give a dismissive, extreme or entirely one-sided response. The question would not have been set if the answer were not debatable. An ability and willingness to see both sides is a high-order skill and shows independence of judgement as a reader. Do not be afraid to explore the issues and do not try to tie the text into one neat interpretation. If there is ambiguity it is likely to be deliberate on the part of the author and must be discussed; literary texts are complex and often paradoxical, and it would be a misreading of them to suggest that there is only one possible interpretation. You are not expected, however, to argue equally strongly or extensively for both sides of an argument, since personal opinion is an important factor. It is advisable to deal with the alternative view at the beginning of your response, and then construct your own view as the main part of the essay. This makes it less likely that you will appear to cancel out your own line of argument.

Although the essay question may ask you to base your answer on one, two or three passages or incidents, you should still refer to other parts of the text where relevant. As long as you stay focused on your main selection of material and on the key words in the question, you will get credit for making brief comments on other supporting material, which could include reference to critical works, works by other authors, or other works by the same author, as well as links to elsewhere in the same text.

Remember that characters do not work in isolation, and a full analysis of a passage usually requires at least passing references to several characters for purposes of comparison and contrast. Don't neglect the minor characters in the text; they may not appear to say or do much, but they must be there for a reason — perhaps to provide useful comments on the main characters, or to represent aspects of themes.

Levels of response

A text can be responded to on four levels, but only the top one can receive the highest marks:

- If you just give a character sketch or account of an incident this is the lowest level, giving evidence of no skill other than being aware of the plotline and characters, which does not even require a reading of the text itself. You are dealing only with the question 'What?' and in a limited context.
- The next level, at about grade D, is a wider or more detailed commentary on plot or characterisation, even making connections between characters and events, but which still doesn't show real understanding of the text or an ability to interpret its themes.
- For a C or low B grade you need to link different areas of the text, enter into discussion and explore major issues, though they may be in isolation from each other. This type of response addresses the question 'Why?'
- A high B or A grade requires you to perform on an analytical level, showing an ability to think conceptually, range across the whole text or deeply into a particular passage. You will be inferring and drawing conclusions based on an overview approached through a grasp of the overall themes which provide the coherent framework for the text. As well as character, plot and theme analysis, you will need to discuss language, style and structural elements and link everything together. The question 'How?' is fully addressed at this level.

Length and timing

You will probably know whether length and timing are problematic areas for you. Although quality matters more than quantity, if you write fewer than three sides of A4 it is unlikely that you will be able to explore fully and give a comprehensive answer to the question. On the other hand, you have only one hour (unless doing an AQA comparative question) — minus planning and checking time — to actually write your essay, so you must practise the planning and writing stages under timed conditions until you are confident that you can give a full answer, ideally four sides, within the time limit and without referring to the text. Finishing too early is not desirable, since the essay is unlikely to be as good as it could have been if the time had been fully utilised. The secret of length/timing success is to have developed a concise style and a brisk pace so that a lot of material is covered in a short space.

Choosing the right question

The first skill you must show when presented with the exam paper is the ability to choose the better, for you, of the two questions on your text where there is a choice. This is not to say you should always go for the same type of essay and if the question is not one which you feel happy with for any reason, you should seriously consider the other, even if it is not the type you normally prefer. It is unlikely but possible that a question contains a word you are not sure you know the meaning of, in which case it would be safer to choose the other one.

Do not be tempted to choose a question because of its similarity to one you have already done. Freshness and thinking on the spot usually produce a better product than attempted recall of a previous essay which may have received only a mediocre mark in the first place. The exam question is unlikely to have exactly the same focus and your response may seem 'off centre' as a result, as well as stale and perfunctory in expression.

Essay questions fall into the following categories: close section analysis and relation to whole text; characterisation; setting and atmosphere; structure and effectiveness; genre; language and style; themes and issues. Remember, however, that themes are relevant to all essays, and that analysis, not just description, is always required.

Underlining key words

When you have chosen your question, underline the key words in the title. There may be only one or as many as five or six, and it is essential that you discover how many aspects your response has to cover and fix in your mind the focus the answer must have. An essay which answers only half of the question cannot score top marks, however well that half is executed, and you need to demonstrate your responsiveness to all the implications of the question. The key words often provide the subheadings for planning and can suggest the overall approach to the essay.

Planning and structuring

To be convincing, your essay must demonstrate a logical order of thought and a sense of progression towards a conclusion. If you reproduce your ideas in random order as they occur to you, they are unlikely to form a coherent whole. Jumping between unrelated ideas is confusing for the reader and weakens the argument. If you find yourself repeating a quotation, or writing 'as I said earlier' or 'as will be discussed later', you have probably not structured your essay effectively. There is no right structure for an essay, as long as there is one.

When planning an essay, which you can afford to spend 7–8 minutes on, your first action should be to brainstorm as a list all the appropriate ideas and material you can think of, in note form and using abbreviations to save time. You should aim for 10–12 separate points — about half a page — which will become the 10 or 12 paragraphs of your essay. If after a few minutes you do not have enough material, quickly switch to the other essay title. Beside each point, in a parallel column, indicate how you will support it. Next, group together the ideas which seem to belong together, and sort them into a logical order, using numbers. Identify which point will be the basis of your conclusion — the one with the overview — and move it to the end. The first points will follow from the essay title and definition of key words, and will be a springboard for your line of argument.

Remember that character, events and aspects of language exist as vehicles for a novel's themes — the real reason why texts are written. You need to become accustomed to planning by theme, using the other three elements to provide support and examples. Material relating to social and historical context needs to be integrated into your response and not just tacked on to the beginning or end.

Avoid running commentaries: texts should not be treated chronologically but according to the argument you construct in answer to the question.

Your plan should be cancelled with one diagonal line when you have finished writing your essay. The examiner does not want to start reading it by mistake, but on the other hand it will be noted that it exists and will raise expectations. Your plan can be flexible — you can add extra material or decide to delete some during the writing stage — but it provides your basic structure and safety net.

Evidence

When selecting a point, check that you can support it adequately and convincingly; if not, substitute a better point. Unsupported assertion does not get much credit in exam essays and gives the impression of desperation or lack of familiarity with the text. Using about three paragraphs to a page, you should structure each paragraph by making a point and then supporting it with textual evidence, and a brief analysis of what it contributes to your overall answer to the question. Evidence for your argument can take three forms: reference, example or quotation. Aim for a mixture of these forms, as well as of different kinds of evidence (character, plot, image etc.). Bear in mind that there is no need to support indisputable facts, for example that Vincentio is Duke of Vienna.

Quotation is not a substitute for thought or argument; it should support your interpretation, and relate directly to the point you are making. It is the most effective way of proving familiarity and confidence in the use of the text, and of validating your claims. When using other people's ideas as support, you must give credit where it is due, rather than trying to pass them off as your own. It rarely fools the examiner and it is much more scholarly to attribute the reference, unless it is something which has been completely absorbed into your own interpretation and expressed in your own words. Otherwise, you can acknowledge source material by paraphrasing or summarising it, or by quoting exactly in inverted commas, mentioning the author in each case. A third option, if you have a quotation or idea you want to include but can't remember exactly where it came from, is to say 'as has been claimed by a critic…' or 'it has been pointed out that…'.

Choose exactly the right quotation for what you are trying to prove, and use only the words from it which you actually need. You can show that you have removed words from a quotation by using the following symbol to replace the missing bit: […]. The cardinal rule is to quote accurately. If in doubt, it is safer to paraphrase than to guess wrongly.

Do not be afraid of using too much quotation; up to a quarter of an essay, or one per sentence, is acceptable. However, quotation for the sake of it, without inter-pretation or relevance, is useless, and you should aim for short, integrated quotations of two or three words rather than longer ones, which take time and space. Short quotations (less than one line of printed text) can be incorporated into your own sentence. Longer quotations need to be introduced by a colon and inset from both margins. If you are considering using such a lengthy quotation, pause and ask yourself if it is all necessary.

If you can't think of the right quotation to prove a point, reconsider whether the point is valid or worth making, or use example or illustration instead. Remember that a quotation may prove more than one point. Rather than repeating it, which weakens its effect, use it as a 'sandwich' between the two ideas it illustrates, which gives the impression of clever planning and structuring.

When making quotations, you do not need to give page, act or scene references. Never give references instead of the quotation; examiners don't have time to look them up and may be using a different edition of the text. Put quotations in inverted commas. Use an underline for the title of the play.

Openings

Openings are the first indication to the examiner of whether you are an excellent, middling or weak student; it will be difficult to correct that first impression. By the end of the first paragraph you will have revealed an ability to write relevantly, accurately, clearly — or not. For the most part, the best way into a literature essay is to define the implications and complexities of the title, starting with the underlined key words, especially if they are abstract concepts with a variety of possible interpretations (such as 'successful' and 'truth'). Next, the widest and broadest application of the terms to the text will produce a range of ideas which could themselves be the structural headings for the essay.

As well as indicating the scope and framework for the answer, the introduction should provide brief and relevant contextual information, including the setting of the scene for a passage question, or the general background for a whole-text answer. This may refer to the genre, the period, the themes or the main characters. It should not, however, be: a full plot synopsis; a summary of the life and work of the author; a repeat of the question; a vague and unfocused comment on life in general; or a list of any kind. Only points directly relevant to the question can be credited, so get started on the analysis as soon as possible. An introduction does not need to be more than a short paragraph and should not be longer than half a page.

Writing

With a useful plan you can write continuously — without needing to stop and think what to say next — and with fluency and coherence. You will need to write quickly and legibly. Think about appropriate expression and accuracy, asking yourself always 'What exactly am I trying to say?' Try to sound engaged and enthusiastic in your response; examiners are human and are affected by tone as much as any reader. It is actually possible to enjoy writing an essay, even in exam conditions! Learn and apply the mnemonic acronym ACRID (accurate, concise, relevant, interesting and detailed).

Each paragraph should follow logically from the one before, either to continue the argument or to change its direction. Adverbial paragraph links — such as 'Furthermore', 'However', 'On the other hand' — are vital pointers to the progression of the argument. Paragraphs are a necessary courtesy to the reader and an indicator of point/topic change; paragraphs which are too long or too short reveal repetitive expression and lack of structure, or undeveloped ideas and lack of support respectively.

Avoid tentative or dogmatic statements, which make you sound either vague and uncertain or pompous and arrogant. Don't overstate or become sensational or emotional; steer clear of cliché and 'waffle'. Use known literary conventions, such as discussing literature in the present tense, avoiding calling a reader 'he', and using the surnames only of authors. In an exam essay, it is usually safer to discuss the text itself, rather than to speculate about the author's intentions or personal viewpoint. Examiners are not looking for an exhaustive list of what you know about the author; they want to see your response to the text, and how you can apply your analysis to the question.

Write in a suitably formal, objective and impersonal style, avoiding ambiguous, repetitive and vague phrases. The aim is always clarity of thought and expression. Use appropriate technical terms to show competence and save words, and choose exactly the right word and not the rough approximation which first comes to mind. Remember that every word should work for you and don't waste time on 'filler' expressions, such as 'As far as the novel is concerned', and adverbial intensifiers, such as 'very' and 'indeed'. Say something once, explore it, prove it and move on; you can only get credit for a point once. You don't need to preface every point with 'I think that' or 'I believe', since the whole essay is supposed to consist of what you think and believe. Don't keep repeating the terms of the title; the whole essay is supposed to be linked to the title, so you don't need to keep saying so. It must always be clear, however, how your point relates to the title, not left to the reader to guess or mind-read what you think the connection may be.

Do not speculate, hypothesise, exaggerate or ask questions — it's your job to answer them. Feelings are not a substitute for thought in an academic essay. 'I feel' is usually a prelude to some unsubstantiated 'gushing'. Do not patronise the author by praising them for being clever or achieving something. Do not parrot your teacher through your marginal notes. The examiner will quickly spot if the whole class is using the same phrases, and will then know it is not your own idea which is being expressed. To quote from examiners' comments, to achieve a grade A, candidates are required to 'show a freshness of personal response as opposed to mere repetition of someone else's critical opinions, however good'. Whether the examiner agrees with you or not is irrelevant; it's the quality of the argument that counts.

Whilst writing, you need to keep an eye on the clock and aim to finish five minutes before the end of the exam to give you checking time. If you find you are running short of time, telescope the argument but try to cover all your points. As an emergency measure, break into notes to show what you would have written. This is worth more than spending your last precious five minutes finishing a particular sentence but not indicating what would have come next if you hadn't miscalculated.

Endings

Endings are as important as openings, and so require an equal amount of thought. They are what the whole essay has been working towards and what the examiner has in mind when deciding upon a final mark. An ending needs to be conclusive, impressive and climactic, and not give the impression that the student has run out of time, ideas or ink. An ineffective ending is often the result of poor planning. Just repeating a point already made or lamely ending with a summary of the essay is a weak way of finishing, and cannot earn any extra marks.

Once again there are techniques for constructing conclusions. You need to take a step back from the close focus of the essay and make a comment which pulls together everything you've been saying and ties it into the overall significance of the text. A quotation from within or outside the text, possibly by a critic, can be effective and definitive. You can also refer back to the title, or your opening statement, so that there is a satisfying sense of circularity for the reader, giving the impression that there is no more to be said on this subject.

Checking

Writing fast always causes slips of the mind and pen, and unfortunately these missing letters and words, misnamings of characters and genre confusions, are indistinguishable from ignorance and therefore must be corrected before submission. Also, you don't want to give away the fact that you didn't bother to check your work, which will give a negative impression of your standards as a literature student. Examiners can always tell when work has been left unchecked.

Allow five minutes for checking your essay. Having spent several months on the study of a text it is worth getting your only exam essay on it as good as you can make it. A few minutes spent checking can make the difference of a grade. Do not be afraid to cross out; neat writing and immaculate presentation are not skills being assessed, but 'accurate and coherent written expression' is. As long as it is done neatly with one line, not a scribble, and the replacement word is written above legibly, correction counts in your favour rather than against you. Insert an asterisk in the text and put a longer addition at the bottom of the essay, rather than trying to cram it into the margin, where it will be difficult to read and which is examiner territory. If you've forgotten to change paragraphs often enough, put in markers (//) when checking to show where a paragraph indentation should be.

When you check, you are no longer the writer but the reader of the text you have created, and a stranger too. Can you follow its line of argument? Are the facts accurate? Does it hang together? Is the vocabulary explicit? Is everything supported? And most importantly, but sadly often not true, does it actually answer the question (even if the answer is that there is no answer)? You also need to watch out for spelling, grammar and punctuation errors, as well as continuing until the last second to improve the content and the expression. Don't waste time counting words.

There is no such thing as a perfect or model essay; flawed essays can gain full marks. There is always something more which could have been said, and examiners realise that students have limitations when writing under pressure in timed conditions. You are not penalised for what you didn't say in comparison to some idealised concept of the perfect answer, but rewarded for the knowledge and understanding you have shown. It is not as difficult as you may think to do well, provided that you know the text in detail and have sufficient essay-writing experience. Follow the process of **choose**, **underline**, **select**, **support**, **structure**, **write** and **check**, and you can't go far wrong.

Text Guidance

Contexts

The England of the early 1600s had just undergone a radical change of monarch and was involved in ambitious ventures of discovery and colonial expansion. The new century brought challenges to the Elizabethan world view inherited from the Middle Ages, and this conflict is represented in the drama of the period.

Cultural context

Below are some of the contemporary religious beliefs and social attitudes that throw light on the hopes, fears, thoughts and actions of the characters in *Measure for Measure*, and that Shakespeare exploits whilst simultaneously calling them into question.

Chain of being

The Elizabethans inherited from medieval theology the concept of a hierarchical chain of being on which every creature appeared in its ordained position on a ladder descending from God through angel, king, man and woman (in that order) to animal, vegetable and finally mineral. It is necessary to know this belief in a divine order to appreciate the objection to women ruling men, and why it was believed that failure to apply reason reduced humans to the animal state of being, governed by appetite and instinct (like Barnardine). In Shakespeare's plays, a human who falls below the level of man into the realm of bestiality is labelled a monster. Many people thought at the time that moral sensibility was a product of social class, i.e. that nobility of behaviour was dependent upon noble birth, and the word 'villain' comes from the Middle English word for peasant.

Divine right of kings

An extension of the concept of feudal hierarchy was a belief in the divine right of kings, whereby rulers considered themselves to be God's anointed deputies on Earth, and therefore higher than ordinary men, and expected to be treated accordingly by their subjects, and on no account usurped, or even criticised. The common people needed kingship to be made visible to men through the trappings of royalty and ceremony, and therefore it is necessary for rule that the ruler does not retire into private life. Angelo, as his name suggests, takes his elevation to dukehood and therefore to divinity very seriously, and cannot resist this opportunity to play God with matters of life and death, as if he is above the law.

Nature

The ubiquitous presence of the word 'Nature' in Elizabethan literature, in addition to imagery deriving from it and arguments about it, stems from the contemporary debate about the definition of Nature, which has two contradictory aspects: the benevolent and harmonious (as portrayed by spring and harvest), and the malevolent and violent (evident in storms, fire and ice). Shakespeare plays with the paradox of the existence of unnatural desires, which could only have been bred by Nature and must, therefore, be natural in some sense. His plays examine closely the concept of human nature and its relationship to Nature as a whole, and in this play procreation is the connecting issue: how can it be both natural and illegal?

Appearance

External appearance was believed by many in Shakespeare's time to be an indicator of what lay within, i.e. goodness or evil. This legacy is still with us, whereby beauty and whiteness are associated with fair, and ugliness and blackness with foul. A physical deformity was thought to be the devil's mark and took many women to the stake. Appearance versus reality is a central issue in *Measure for Measure*, and the imagery of 'seeming' permeates the language of this and many other Shakespeare plays. If appearances, which are all we have to go on, are deceptive, and therefore character judgement is false, knowledge erroneous and truth elusive, then one cannot be sure of anything. This is the conundrum which torments many of Shakespeare's heroes, usually with tragic consequences. In *Measure for Measure*, the 'seemer' Angelo is revealed before it is too late. The Elizabethans believed that temptation could take the form of an angel who was really a devil in disguise.

Reason

The failure of reason was considered to be the cause of the Fall of Man (Adam allowed his love for Eve to overrule his better judgement and obedience to God), and Elizabethans therefore believed it was dangerous to let reason be dominated by passion. Characters in Shakespeare's plays who become uncontrollably emotional are heading for a fall, as their intellect is what makes them human (superior to beasts) and keeps them sane. Angelo, like Othello, gives his 'sensual race the rein' (II.4.160) and this is the downward turning point for him. In a state of heightened passion, such as desire, mistakes are made, impulses are activated without sufficient reflection to moderate them, and one is no longer in control of oneself or of the situation.

The seven deadly sins

The seven deadly sins of the medieval church were pride, envy, gluttony (greed), lechery (lust), avarice (love of money), wrath (anger) and sloth (laziness). These vices (which can be identified in literary works until at least the mid-nineteenth century) were the foundation of morality in the medieval and Elizabethan/Jacobean periods. They feature as a masque in Marlowe's *Doctor Faustus*, for instance. Shakespeare employs them as a means of suggesting the faults of heroes and villains alike, with Angelo (and a large part of the population of Vienna) guilty of lechery, Isabella and Angelo of pride, and Barnardine of sloth and possibly wrath (since he is a murderer). These mortal sins were believed to consign one's soul to hell unless repented of.

Hell and damnation

The fear of damnation and hell apparent in the works of Shakespeare and his fellow playwrights stems from a contemporary conviction that there literally was such a place below ground, inhabited by tormented souls allowed to walk the earth between midnight and dawn. Hell was typically portrayed as engulfed in dark flames fuelled by sulphur (brimstone) to torture human flesh. The Elizabethans also believed in diabolic possession and the incarnation of the devil in human form. Women were feared because their beauty gave them power to ensnare men's souls.

Chastity

Students might wonder at the insistence on female chastity in this and so many of Shakespeare's plays. The security of society and peace of mind of men was dependent upon women's virginity before marriage — making them a bargaining tool for advantageous marriages to benefit the father's social status — and chastity after it, meaning faithfulness to their husbands. In a society which passes inheritance down the male line, men needed to be sure that their son was really their own and not someone else's bastard, and a man's reputation would be destroyed by an unfaithful wife. Virginity and chastity were linked to religion via the Virgin Mary and regarded not only as an ideal state for women but as a test of the nobility of males, since only the higher orders were thought to be able to resist the temptations of the flesh. There is no suggestion that the Duke finds Isabella sexually attractive; rather he is drawn to her because of her virtuousness. The words used to define women, then and until recently, all relate to their sexual, and therefore financial, relationship with men: virgin, wife, widow, whore; the Duke tells Mariana 'Why, you are nothing then. Neither maid, widow, nor wife?' (V.1.177–78). Females belonged in one of two extreme categories, then and for many centuries later: despised whore or venerated angel, depending on their sexual activity, or what others said about it; a woman's reputation was everything.

Spousals and dowries

The practice of spousals (see *Arden* introduction, p. lviii) was common at the time. Claudio and Juliet's marital agreement is a 'true contract' (I.2.144) recognised in common law as a marriage which was binding and could not be breached without legal consequences. They lacked only the blessing of the church ('denunciation of outward order', I.2.147–48) to make their union valid to the state, and there is no reason to doubt that this intention would have been fulfilled in due course, when hcr 'friends' had been brought round and persuaded to release her dowry. In Jacobean eyes Mariana and Angelo are also already morally man and wife, having sworn a declaration of intention, and this partnership only requires cohabitation to gain legal recognition, despite the dowry condition not having been met.

A dowry for the bride was traditional then, and in many countries still is (including in the UK, where the father of the bride is expected to pay for the wedding). The thinking was that since the bride would have to be kept by her future husband — being neither trained nor allowed to work and unable to contribute to the family economy — she should therefore bring a large sum of money, or property, to her marriage. If the father were no longer alive, the obligation to provide a dowry fell upon the eldest son and brother. When Angelo refuses to marry Mariana because her dowry has been lost at sea, this is a common enough reaction to the discovery of an intended bride's lack of promised wealth. He is only criticised for besmirching her reputation as his excuse for not honouring the betrothal. Women who had no family to support them, and no dowry with which to procure a husband, had little alternative but to turn to prostitution, or the church.

Nunneries

Entry into a nunnery was a method of disposing of unwanted, superfluous or disgraced daughters, who did not choose to go but were sent, or was a refuge for women with no financial means. However, voluntary withdrawal from the world on religious grounds was viewed differently, and sometimes seen as unnatural, or a self-indulgence, or neglect of the duty to find a husband and produce sons to ensure the continuity of the family line.

Silence

Silence was considered a desirable and appropriate virtue for a woman, whether a nun or no, since society did not deem her to be sufficiently intelligent or educated to have anything worth saying, especially in male company. The misogynistic medieval church preached that Eve brought about Adam's and all mankind's downfall by speaking out of turn and seducing him with words (in the same way as Satan had seduced her). It therefore befitted the guilt of the daughters of Eve that they should be meek and obedient, as best demonstrated by silence. Nuns had to refuse to show their face to visitors if they wished to speak to them (I.4.12–13) to limit their effect on and power over men. Garrulity was associated with sexual licentiousness (as epitomised by Chaucer's Wife of Bath) and there are many examples in literature of the figure of the silent or silenced woman.

Puritanism

The extreme religious faction of Puritanism was a growing phenomenon at the beginning of the seventeenth century, as Shakespeare knew to his cost. The theatre was one of the main targets of the philistine movement; play-acting was banned in the City of London in 1596 and dramatists were forced to operate in Southwark, where audiences were smaller and therefore less profitable. Angelo and Isabella both represent the unattractive excesses of puritan belief — rigidity and sanctimoniousness (which so easily degenerates into hypocrisy when the superhuman ideals cannot be lived up to). Puritans were often attracted by the life removed, the private world of study cut off from the temptations of the public world of the flesh (what Milton called 'a fugitive and cloister'd virtue' in *Areopagitica*). But although erudition and piety were generally respected at the time, the abdication of duty by those of rank was considered a moral and social failing which led to civil disorder. Weak rule was the greatest fear of the Elizabethan/Jacobean generation, who had seen too many examples of its horrific consequences.

Historical context

War and politics

The Vienna of the early seventeenth century was the capital city both of Austria and of the Holy Roman Empire. It also constituted the frontier between Europe and the forces of disorder to the east, exemplified by the Hungarians (descendants of the fabled Huns), the Russians and the Muslim Ottoman Empire. A long war against the Hungarian king had been fought in the late fifteenth century, and the Ottomans had besieged the city in 1529. There are references in Act I scene 2 of the play to the Holy Wars with Hungary (the setting of the source play *Promos and Cassandra*) and in Act III scene 2 to the 'Emperor of Russia' and Rome to account for the Duke's disappearance. In fact, all political references in the play can be accounted for by the events and treaty negotiations with Spain, England's old enemy, of the winter of 1603–04 and spring and summer of 1604. However, Spain could not be directly referred to as the censor objected to the discussion of current foreign affairs on the stage (see *Arden* introduction, p. xxxi).

On the other hand, leaving aside specific references, the play emphasises that war is an unnatural and extreme state for any country to be in and is traditionally used as an excuse for illegality and immorality, since in times of war 'quite athwart/Goes all decorum' (I.3.30–31). Home affairs are neglected when more urgent ones of state security and foreign policy demand a ruler's full attention. The same background of war and external threat occurs in many of Shakespeare's tragedies, including *Othello* and *Hamlet*. There is always a group of citizens, high and low, who benefit from war and lament peace because it reduces their opportunities and income. Such is Lucio the mercenary soldier, and Mistress Overdone and her crew, who are now 'custom-shrunk' (I.2.83).

Disease and lawlessness

The Vienna of the play is near in practice but distant in geography from Jacobean London, so could be safely commented on and relevantly satirised. London too had its idle fops, its devious politicians, its criminal underworld and an appetite for lechery and laxity which made the rising Puritans call for a new severity to combat 'too much liberty' (I.2.124) and to deplore the growth of vice manifest in the proliferation of brothels and gaming-houses. A stronger penalty than fines or standing in a white sheet was believed necessary as a deterrent to lewd offences, and Puritan extremists demanded the death penalty.

Vienna is diseased, actually and metaphorically. Too much licence has made it lawless and tainted, its liberalism exploited even by those who should be the enforcers of standards and rules. It is a place of misrule with the uncertainty which comes with an abdication of leadership and a disrespect for the law. Life on the streets is decadent and degenerate, overrun and threatened by an underclass that inhabits taverns and brothels, and who have no decorum in their habits, tastes and relationships. Authority and hierarchy are debased equally by the higher orders, who practise duplicity and hide corruption behind sanctimoniousness. In such a place the stupid Master Froths are gulled, the Isabellas decide to retreat to nunneries, the Barnardines become murderers, and the Lucios see nothing wrong in slandering their Duke. Chaos is come again, and chaos is the work of the devil, requiring a God to restore harmony, order and rationality.

There was plague in London in the winter of 1603–04, which necessitated the pulling down of slum houses in the suburbs and was responsible for a slackness of trade in the capital. A proclamation of 16 September 1603 warned against the spread of the disease by 'dissolute and idle persons', which would seem a fitting description of Lucio and his associates.

Sex and punishment

Sex before or outside of wedlock was commonplace in Elizabethan and Jacobean England, and illicit liaisons were frequent among courtiers and royalty, as was the contracting of 'the pox' (syphilis). Illegitimacy, however, was necessarily a stigma in a period when religious observance was a test of nobility and when the laws of succession and inheritance depended upon sons and heirs of their father's bloodline. (*King Lear* deals with the social destabilisation caused by sons conceived outside the marital bed. The bastard Edmund is sent out of the country for nine years by the Earl of Gloucester in an attempt to avoid scandal.) So in London as in Vienna, common practice and acknowledged mores were at odds with the ideals of religion and state.

According to Lawrence Stone in *The Family, Sex and Marriage in England 1500–1800,* society in England at the turn of the sixteenth century was sexually lax but highly inquisitorial. There was a huge number of prosecutions in church courts for sexual offences of all kinds between 1558 and 1603, two of which — buggery and bestiality — carried the death penalty. The parish took a severe view of the consequences of irregular sex, i.e. bastard children, because they were a drain on public resources. Until as late as 1700 both mother and father were often stripped and whipped through the streets.

The world of Vienna in the play is one where weakness is in danger of turning to evil, but where the supposed remedy may be more deadly than the disease.

Theatrical context

Shakespeare and contemporary theatre

In the early seventeenth century, when Shakespeare wrote his major tragedies and later comedies, drama had generally become more political, satirical, dark and violent compared to the more lyrical tastes and pastoral works of the Elizabethans. There was a growing fashion for the use of masque and spectacle in plays and poetry, and an emphasis on bloodthirsty revenge tragedies in urban settings among fellow playwrights such as Ben Jonson and John Webster. However, wit, irony and sophistication of ideas were still paramount in the plots, characterisation and language of the theatre. Play-going appealed to all sections of the population; the poor stood as 'groundlings' below the raised stage, whilst the wealthier sat in galleries or boxes. King James was a keen theatre-goer and supporter of Shakespeare's company, The King's Men, with a personal interest in witchcraft, religion, morality and the role of the monarch. Contemporary playwrights catered for these tastes in their choice of subject matter and creation of characters.

Morality plays

Morality plays were **allegorical** dramatic works popular in Europe during the medieval period, in which the characters personify moral qualities (such as charity or envy) or abstractions (such as death or youth) and in which moral lessons are taught. They featured an Everyman figure being subjected to temptation as a test of his virtue by a Vice figure whose aim was to win his soul for the devil. A London audience of the first decade of the seventeenth century expected similar punishment for transgression to those of the medieval era, and their guilty consciences could be activated by visions of the torments of hell, by the threat of the ruthless Inquisition, by examples of suffering for one's sins, and by reminders of the consequences of repentance left too late, as in Marlowe's *Doctor Faustus*.

Comedy characteristics

The Penguin editor presents a case for *Measure for Measure* being a romantic comedy similar to *Much Ado About Nothing*, whereby the couple (the Duke and Isabella) start off being too confident in their own and others' qualities, and have to learn that they, and all human beings, are in fact flawed. They acquire wisdom, charity and human understanding through traumatic experience; through learning to know themselves, each other and their fellow men they are able to shed false values (introduction, p. 34). The play contains several references to the taking of vows and the giving of promises, which are a feature of fairytales and therefore of romantic comedies. Typically of Shakespeare's comedies, the play ends with three marriages being arranged.

As in many of Shakespeare's comedies, the play has a parallel plot, in this case one whereby Angelo and Mariana's betrothal can be compared with Claudio and Juliet's. The play employs two comedy conventions involving disguise and substitution: the 'head trick' and the 'bed trick' or the 'maidenhead trick', a well-known folk plot device also used in *All's Well That Ends Well*. Two other traditional plot components are in the form of the corrupt magistrate and the disguised ruler. Earlier versions of the corrupt magistrate story ended with his having to marry the widow of the man he has put to death to restore her lost honour, and then his being executed immediately afterwards as a double act of justice.

Play context

It is widely assumed that Shakespeare never left England, though the majority of his plays in all genres are set in other countries. Italian city-states were particularly favoured by Shakespeare and his contemporaries because, thanks to **Machiavelli**, they were synonymous with ruthless politics and the origin of not only the Renaissance but of many of the source texts which inspired Elizabethan and Jacobean playwrights. Foreign settings also have the advantage of allowing comments on local political and social issues to be made circumspectly, as in *Measure for Measure*. Note that this play is a rare exception for Shakespeare in being set somewhere other than in the Mediterranean or in Britain.

Measure for Measure was presented to the court in the banqueting hall at Whitehall on Boxing Day 1604 by the newly formed King's Men, and therefore was probably written (and possibly previously acted) in the summer of that year. *Measure for Measure* falls between *Hamlet* and *Othello*, and therefore shares something of the ideas and mood of these two works. Certain early Jacobean plays, ostensibly comedies, are 'charged with a weight of moral and social preoccupations' (*Arden* introduction, p. lv). The Penguin editor has pronounced that 'this play fails to rank among Shakespeare's supremely great achievements' (introduction, p. 45), but it nonetheless advances the questions posed by the great tragedies and foreshadows answers given in the final romances, and therefore occupies a unique place in the Shakespeare canon.

Reign of James I

Shakespeare and his company were honoured by the new monarch in being patronised and allowed to adopt the name of The King's Men. The plays of the first years of James's reign are characterised by a profound questioning, but also by stronger affirmations than in Elizabethan times. They are intensely concerned with the nature of authority. King James's treatise on kingship, *Basilikon Doron*, is proposed as a model for Shakespeare's presentation of the Duke by some commentators, and disputed by others.

James I has been described as 'a Living Library, and a walking Study' (see *Arden* introduction, p. xlviii). Like Duke Vincentio, and Prospero in *The Tempest*, he spent many hours in bookish seclusion, and he admitted to having been too lax and having governed too leniently at the beginning of his reign (*Arden* introduction, p. xlix). He made a would-be secret visit to the Exchange in March 1604 with the intention of watching the merchants while remaining unobserved, which suggests an inspiration for Shakespeare's spying duke of dark corners. James was also given to showy *coups de théâtre* in the form of the whimsical dispensing of last-minute pardons to condemned prisoners on the scaffold (like Barnardine) and other arbitrary acts of 'justice'. He disliked crowds and adulation, and had a paranoia about slander (an offence he had made punishable by death in Scotland). It has been remarked that 'the character of the Duke is a very accurate delineation of that of King James, which Shakespeare appears to have caught with great felicity and to have sketched with much truth' (George Chalmers, 1799).

Model rulers

In his book defining his beliefs on wise government and the responsibilities of rulers, James I comes across as the archetypal Renaissance prince. Several passages in *Measure for Measure* paraphrase parts of *Basilikon Doron* (meaning 'the gift of kings'). Another inspirational figure for Shakespeare is believed to have been that of Maximilian, Holy Roman Emperor (whose seat as a Hapsburg duke of Austria was in Vienna), who was held up as a pattern to all rulers for his blending of justice and mercy (*Arden* introduction, p. xl). Another candidate was the Roman Emperor Alexander Severus (*Arden* introduction, p. xliv), who according to popular belief used to disguise himself in various guises in order to listen to complaints and right the wrongs of his people. The Duke can be seen at least partly as an amalgam of the qualities of Severus and Maximian, another Roman Emperor, as presented by sixteenth-century writers.

Sources

Shakespeare used known sources for 35 of his 37 plays, and it is assumed that the other two must have had sources as yet undiscovered. Up to this time, and for some time after (until the aptly named novel in the early eighteenth century in fact), originality of plot or character was not considered necessary or even desirable in literary works; a largely illiterate population and a traditional oral culture created a demand for the familiar and reassuring, as with children and their bedtime stories. Audiences expected to already know the basic storylines, settings and outcomes of plays they attended, and the skill and creativity of the playwright was demonstrated by the quality of the improvements made to an existing work, including the adaptation of the genre.

Measure for Measure has a folktale plot often treated by earlier writers. Shakespeare's main sources were a novella by the Italian writer Geraldo Cinthio (also a source for *Othello*), and a ten-act play by George Whetstone called *Promos and Cassandra*. The Penguin editor (commentary, p. 155) also points out that much of *Measure for Measure* is derived from the Sermon on the Mount. Cinthio told the tale in his collection of prose tales *Hecatommithi*, meaning one hundred tales, published in Sicily in 1565, and repeated it in a tragedy entitled *Epitia* (1583). In Cinthio's version, the eponymous heroine is a young virgin, the sister rather than the wife of the condemned man (as she is in *Promos and Cassandra)*. The commuting of the death sentence on the plea of Epitia combined justice with mercy, providing a Christian ethic rather than the classical nemesis of his own source stories.

Whetstone's play *The Right Excellent and Famous Historye of Promos and Cassandra,* set in Hungary in 1578, was subsequently turned into a novella in 1582. It is exceedingly long and its dialogue is dull, but its preoccupation with moral philosophy and received values interested Shakespeare and he seized upon them and enriched them. It is concerned with the doctrine of universal order fallen into decay through moral anarchy, as also treated in *Hamlet. Promos and Cassandra* is closer in structure to *Measure for Measure* and has many direct parallels (see *Arden* introduction, p. xliii), including a lowlife, comic subplot. Shakespeare simplified the elaborate settings and moved the play to Vienna from Hungary, removed many of the minor characters, changed the names, made Angelo a more complex personality, and introduced the Duke, Lucio, Mariana, Escalus, Abhorson and Barnardine. Generally there is more subtlety and complexity in Shakespeare's version, mostly created by the fact that Isabella refuses to sacrifice her honour, and by the activities of the Duke which transform the play from a simple tale of legal/sexual blackmail into a profound political parable about morality and justice. This is a summary of the source story from *Promos and Cassandra* (Penguin introduction, pp. 14–15).

…in the Hungarian city of Julio, the laws against fornication, which had long since been disregarded, are invoked with extreme severity against a certain Andrugio by the King's deputy, Promos. When Andrugio's beautiful and virtuous sister Cassandra intercedes Promos temporarily relents, but subsequently makes the reprieve conditional upon her surrendering her body to him. She refuses at first, but is afterwards persuaded by Andrugio's pleas and assents to Promos's terms, provided that he will first pardon her brother and then marry her. Promos thereupon has intercourse with her, but repudiates his promises and orders a gaoler to present Cassandra with the severed head of Andrugio. The gaoler substitutes the mangled head of a newly executed felon, which Cassandra takes to be that of her brother. She straightway informs the King, who rules that Promos shall first marry Cassandra and then be beheaded. As soon as the marriage has been solemnized, however, she discovers that she genuinely loves him and pleads for his life to be spared. This the King refuses until Andrugio, who has been present in disguise, reveals himself; both he and Promos are then granted a free pardon.

Quiller-Couch (*The New Shakespeare* introduction, p. xvi) says that the source story is 'tedious, flat, stale and unprofitable; whereas *Measure for Measure*, for all its flaws, is alive, interesting, exciting, in parts powerfully — even terrifically — moving; and the secret of its difference lies in its poetry — in that and in nothing else'. R. W. Chambers summarises the changes (Muir, p. 107) as 'removing its morbid details, harmonising its crudities, giving humanity and humour to its low characters, turning it into a consistent tale of intercession for sin, repentance from and forgiveness of crime'.

The printed text

No manuscripts of any of Shakespeare's plays have survived. Some of the plays were published during his lifetime, in editions known as 'Quarto' from the size of the paper used. Seven years after his death, a collected edition known as the First Folio was published in 1623, which contains all Shakespeare's plays except *Pericles*. Although the Folio is generally considered to be more reliable than the Quartos, for each play the case has to be considered on its merits. We know that Shakespeare often revised the texts of his plays, and often made deletions, and there is no consensus as to which is the more genuine or reliable text. Since he rarely provided even stage localities, a lot has been left to the discretion of editors through the ages. Divisions into acts and scenes, and stage directions, were the responsibility of the copyist and not part of the original script. In the case of *Measure for Measure*, it seems that the original copy was not the theatre prompt book but, more problematically, an untidy draft which had suffered some deterioration. The text as it stands contains some of Shakespeare's most notorious **cruces** and unconvincing substitutions, and a paucity of stage directions.

Measure for Measure appears as the fourth play in the Comedies section of the 1623 Folio. It is generally believed to have been first performed 20 years earlier, at court before King James I on 26 December 1604, since it is thus recorded in the Revels Accounts as *Mesur for Mesur*. It is possible, however, that it was performed earlier in that year, in the summer months (see *Arden* introduction, p. xxxi), based on references to contemporary political events and peace treaties: a proclamation was issued in September 1603 for the pulling down of houses to prevent the spread of plague; James I made a coronation progress through England in the spring of 1603 in which he allegedly manifested a dislike of English popular acclaim as distinct from the quiet appreciation of the Scots (see *Arden* introduction, p. xxxiv).

Textual problems

Measure for Measure, like *Romeo and Juliet*, is a play for which the Folio text is the earliest authority, and is deemed unreliable and yet tantalising for this reason. There are no Quartos for verification and elucidation, and many editors and critics over the centuries have commented on the widespread anomalies and obvious corruptions they have found in the text. These include the creakings of the plot, the faulty condition of some of the passages, the misplaced, missing or superfluous words, and the high proportion of missing exits. Some of these may be attributable to a series of successive revisions, including cutting and expansion, over a period of several years, but it seems indisputable that the Folio text was ultimately based on 'foul papers' or a 'rough draft', and unfortunately there are no parallel texts for comparison.

As in its near contemporary, *Othello*, there is a double time scheme. The imminent execution of Claudio is dealt with in a counting down of time which is completely absent from the comedy scenes where time is vague and elastic. Pompey is rearrested only a day after Claudio's sentencing according to the main time scheme, yet he has had the opportunity to reoffend several times (see *Arden* introduction, p. xiv). The Duke must be absent from Vienna long enough for it to be conceivable that he has travelled to Poland (I.3.14), and for him to have sent several letters to Angelo, but not so long that his absence causes concern among the populace. A list of time discrepancies is given in the *Arden* introduction (p. xv), which mostly concern the hour of Claudio's execution, and a confusing of day and night. It is also unclear whether the laws of Venice have not been applied for 'nineteen zodiacs' (I.2.167) or 'fourteen years' (I.3.21). The silence of Isabella in the last hundred lines is viewed as evidence of either a textual corruption or a strange heedlessness. Most critics agree that there is a break in the play before the last two acts which show signs of haste and carelessness. In Act III scene 1 the Duke starts speaking prose, and the texture and tension of the writing suffers.

Whichever edition you use, a number of changes will have been made from the original text. Different editors often have different views and arrive at different conclusions. The changes and arguments for them are usually indicated in the textual notes. Generally, the goal of an editor is to produce an edition which makes sense when acted on the stage, rather than giving an account of all the possible interpretations of the play.

Problem play?

Measure for Measure has been defined by various critics as a problem play, which means that it does not fit comfortably into any of the three categories of Shakespeare play: **comedy**, history or **tragedy**. Swinburne called it 'a great indefinable poem or unclassifiable play'. It is, however, classified as a comedy in the Folio, and it does fulfil the genre requirements: a triple marriage, a **dénouement**, a final reconciliation and the fact that no one dies. Yet there is a consensus among critics that it has unresolved issues and, therefore, problems of interpretation. The group regarded and labelled as the problem plays, which includes *All's Well That Ends Well* and *Troilus and Cressida,* is also referred to as the dark comedies, because they have no real feeling of satisfaction, celebration or resolution at the end, and considerable disquiet along the way in terms of tone and atmosphere. Until recently, *Measure for Measure* was not much produced, because of its preoccupation with bawdiness (seen paradoxically as both too realistic and too unrealistic to be acceptable). It is in every sense a dark play: death averted but only at the last moment, strong imagery of hell and damnation in the afterlife, and society examined and found wanting in this life. The inhumane behaviour of some characters, even by those we are apparently asked to admire, is difficult to excuse.

The specific complaints against the play concern Isabella's silence at the end, and Angelo and Lucio's reluctance to go along with their determined fates, which makes the atmosphere of the ending very different from that of the earlier comedies. The state of Vienna is still unreformed with no obvious way forward, and there is no convenient transition back to another more normal and more controllable world as occurs in *A Midsummer Night's Dream* (1595) or *As You Like It* (1599). It starts in the mood of a tragedy and its deviation into a comic ending is not totally convincing. Critics are particularly exercised by the change of emotion and language in Act III scene 1. 'Much has been written in defence of the second half of *Measure for Measure*, but it is surely a muddle', both 'prosy and incredible' (Kermode, p. 164). There are many fraught exchanges between pairs of characters — Angelo and Isabella, Isabella and Claudio, Lucio and the Duke — which work against a comedy atmosphere. So too do the extremes of characterisation: there is nothing between the ideal and noble and the base and vile.

Quiller-Couch sees the play's problem (introduction to *The New Shakespeare*, p. xxxi) as Shakespeare's 'failure to make Isabella a consistent character', and Rossiter concludes 'Shakespeare's fault lies in giving Isabella no transitions' (*Fifteen Lectures on Shakespeare*, p. 162). It has also been claimed that the motivation of other characters is unrealistic, particularly that of the Duke. Even the comic elements have been seen as unconvincing and unacceptable: 'of this play the light or comick part is very natural and pleasing, but the grave scenes…have more labour than elegance. The plot is rather intricate than artful' (Dr Johnson, quoted in introduction to *The*

New Shakespeare, p. xiii). Coleridge wholly damned it: 'The comic and tragic parts equally border on the hateful, the one disgusting, the other horrible.'

There is a further structural problem: unnecessary characters abound in *Measure for Measure* and are cited as evidence of lax construction and lack of revision. Justice speaks ten trivial words at the end of Act II scene 1 and appears to be redundant, along with Varrius and the Friars; as Dr Johnson noted, Thomas and Peter could well have been merged into one and may in fact have been intended to be one and the same. In some cases this can be explained by the need for the character left on stage to have someone to talk to while another, for example the Provost, goes off to carry out an instruction necessary to the development of the plot, and for time to appear to have passed, for example in Act II scene 1. Another anomaly is one of missing exits, and also of unnecessary ones where withdrawing but remaining on stage is required for the sense and the action.

One could interpret the movement from tragedy to comedy within the same play as an allegory of the process of redemption. However, the play's moral message that the end justifies the means is dubious at best. Kermode (p. 164) claims: 'The true theme of the play is tragic; as a tragicomedy it fails because the contrivances of the poet too much resemble those of the Duke.' However, it is not really tragic either, because the evil can be described as error, which all frail humanity and flesh is heir to, and it has either occurred before the play begins or it is potential rather than actual. The play is therefore ultimately guilty of being neither one thing nor the other.

Critical history

Illicit sex was not an issue which the seventeenth- to nineteenth-century British respectable classes happily confronted, and even now *Measure for Measure* is hailed as a provocative play of sexual morals. There is also something distasteful about the careless creating, bartering, selling and disposing of bodies which goes on in the play, involving the Provost, Claudio, Isabella, Angelo, Mariana and the Duke, as well as the sex workers for whom it is their means of living. It is therefore traditionally viewed as one of Shakespeare's most difficult and controversial plays, and one lacking in humanity, though this is one of the very topics it explores.

Until this century, *Measure for Measure* was one of those Shakespeare plays with which audiences and critics could not seem to come to terms, and it would not be unfair to say that it was positively unpopular, or, as the Penguin editor puts it, 'its popularity was extraordinarily spasmodic' (introduction, p. 10). In the last few decades, however, its reputation has risen as prudery has waned, and there have been a myriad of productions, most of them set in different cities thought to have had parallel problems in more recent times, for example decadent 1930s Berlin. Modern criticism has brought to light significances and **allegories** which the play had never been thought to possess, particularly in relation to the shifting values and political policies of the late twentieth and early twenty-first centuries. Equally, some critics think the play has been overvalued, especially when it is compared to Shakespeare's great tragedies and late plays. Though it is now continually performed and often present on exam specifications, the play is still commonly viewed as problematic and devoid of characters with whom the audience can fully sympathise; the only humour in the play is unsophisticated and belongs to the lower classes. A modern perspective also makes it difficult to identify with the theological issues of redemption and chastity which underpin Angelo's and Isabella's dilemmas.

According to the prevailing fashion of the age, the play has been variously deemed to be about human morality and sexuality, a social satire, a Christian allegory, a painful and personal quest for truth, or a study of the relationship between the individual and the state. It lends itself to feminist interpretations of hostility to females in a male-ordered universe, as well as to political ones of intrigue behind closed doors and corruption and cynicism in the corridors of power. Religious fanaticism and capital punishment, with prisoners on death row, are still topical causes of debate and concern in many parts of the world.

The critical (in both senses of the word) issues are whether Isabella's decision can be condoned, or even pardoned, and whether the Duke has taken an acceptable risk in absconding and abandoning his flock, especially when he seems to have done so knowingly to a 'seemer'. Critics and audiences also worry about the use of forced marriage to right wrongs of despoiled reputations, and its chances of success. (But it must be remembered that until as late as the mid-nineteenth century it was believed and expounded in literature that a devout woman could cure her future husband of his excesses and make a decent citizen and husband out of him.) In addition to the gender issues, critics are bothered by the class ones: though perhaps a world of Lucios and Pompeys would be more humane and kindly to each other than one consisting of Isabellas, Angelos and Dukes.

The play has always aroused conflicting responses, but it is worth bearing in mind that tastes and intellectual fashions change. In the eighteenth century Dr Johnson found 'the light or comick part very natural and pleasing' but objected that the serious scenes were too contrived and showed 'more labour than elegance' (*The Plays of William Shakespeare*, 1768). A short time later, however, Coleridge found the comic elements 'disgusting' and the serious scenes 'horrible', and condemned this as the most painful of all Shakespeare's dramas. His contemporary, Hazlitt, found the play pleasingly unconventional in its moral stance and all-embracing in its human sympathy, whereas Christian critics have been heart-warmed by its conventional Christian message of the redemption of sin through mercy.

In the nineteenth century the Victorians did not understand Angelo; strangely, given that hypocrisy, especially sexual hypocrisy, is considered by many to be a Victorian vice. In any case its overtly sexual content would have made it unpalatable to audiences in the century of Dr **Bowdler** and the sanitisation of literature. In the early twentieth century the play was seen as evidence of the disturbed spirit and growing scepticism and pessimism of its author, or worse, his own weariness, cynicism and self-disgust and that of the Jacobean age generally. In the 1930s, this biographical approach was dropped by the critical movement in favour of seeing the play as profoundly Christian. Outlined by G. Wilson Knight in *The Wheel of Fire* (1930), a theory was evolved in which *Measure for Measure* was an allegory of divine retribution and atonement, whereby the Duke was Christ descending to judge mankind, Lucio was the eternal adversary, and Isabella was the bride of Christ. One could thereby explain **tragedy** turning into **comedy** as an **allegory** of the process of redemption.

However, Frank Kermode and others later disagreed. In the late twentieth century it was pointed out that nothing was clear-cut enough to be allegorical, given that there is so much ambiguity about both the Duke and Lucio, as well as Isabella. Lucio is oddly useful to both Isabella and Claudio, and to the working out of the comic resolution and the purposes of the Duke, which makes it difficult to sustain a view that he is simply the devil incarnate. And if the Duke is proved to lack omniscience, omnipotence and infallibility (see *Arden* introduction, p. lvii), then he cannot convincingly take on the mantle of the Incarnate Lord.

The fact seems to be that *Measure for Measure* cannot be made to conform to only one approach without damage to others: erring humanity cannot be made to fit doctrinal rigidity or allegorical drama without neglecting certain other aspects of the play. Contemporary verdicts usually settle upon the general term of 'flawed masterpiece', and if it is performed more now than in previous centuries it is usually with a period change to point out a political, moral or social tale. Recently it has become associated with the topical issue of 'sleaze' and has thus become a play for our times. The jury is still out and the debate rages among teachers, students, critics and audiences over the quality of the play. However, the verdict of at least one critic is that '*Measure for Measure* is a great play — in parts, and in despite that its parts do not fit. It arrests — it impresses while it puzzles — every reader' (introduction to *The New Shakespeare*, p. xli). Some of the language is worthy of *Hamlet*, as is the range of humanity presented, from pageboys singing like cherubs in gardens at twilight to murderers growling in straw-filled cells.

Verse and prose

The rhythms of the language are the music of the play, and have the same relaxing or warning effect as sound-tracks in films. Verse is language which is rhythmically organised according to particular patterns of metre and the arrangement of lines. Verse is always poetry, but poetry is not always in verse, although it usually was until comparatively recently. Prose is discourse which is not constructed according to any measurable pattern and is not set out in lines, but which can still have a rhythm.

In plays of Shakespeare's time and earlier, verse was the conventional medium of all literary discourse, including drama, and his plays all consist largely of **blank** (unrhymed) **verse**. Plays were not regarded as naturalistic slices of life, and the heightened language of verse was felt to be appropriate to their non-realistic status as performance texts. However, dramatists increasingly varied the range of their dramatic language to include some speeches and scenes in prose — the language of everyday speech and writing.

Verse tended to be given to noble and royal characters, expressing romantic or elevated feelings, and at certain heightened moments they use **rhyming couplets**. These are also used at the ends of scenes to give them an air of finality — often sinister — or for spells, songs or some other special form of discourse. Couplets also suggest common wisdom is being quoted, as at the end of Act III when the Duke is giving sententious advice. While pentameters are the norm, shorter lines may serve to end a speech, or indicate a pause or hesitation, and 11-syllabled lines, of which there are several in Act II scene 4, have a rhetorical or theatrical effect.

By the start of Shakespeare's career, one particular verse metre had come to dominate the language of plays. This was based on a line of ten syllables, arranged so that the beats, or stresses, fell on every second syllable. Thus each line consisted of five units (or metrical feet), each consisting of an unstressed syllable followed by a stressed one. Each of these units is called an iambic foot, and since there are five of them in each line, the metre is called **iambic pentameter**. Here are two regular examples from the play:

> ~ / ~ / ~ / ~ / ~ /
> We cannot weigh our brother with ourself.

> ~ / ~ / ~ / ~ / ~ /
> The tempter, or the tempted, who sins most?

However, the monotony of several hours of blank verse is avoided by metrical irregularities, incomplete and shared lines, **enjambement, caesuras** and stress reversals. These all obscure the normal verse rhythm and give variety, so that the audience is not usually conscious of the play's dialogue being mainly in verse. Close analysis of the verse reveals that these techniques, as well as having a dramatic effect, can indicate the characters' attitudes and feelings. It is always significant and needs to be interpreted if a character who normally uses verse switches to prose and vice versa, and characters who suddenly become less fluent, inarticulate, incapable of speaking in a smooth rhythm or of finishing a line are often undergoing emotional disturbance or rapid thinking. This is particularly noticeable in Isabella's and Claudio's speeches in Act III scene 1, for example ''Tis best that thou diest quickly'.

Prose was generally reserved for characters of lower social status, for comic or domestic scenes, or to indicate secrecy or conspiracy. Students should be aware of the prose sequences in the play and the effect created by their contrast with what precedes and follows in each case. They also need to note which characters rarely use or are uncomfortable with prose and which change according to their inter-locutor or context, like the Duke. Lucio (like Iago in *Othello*) moves easily between verse and prose, as one would expect, given his fluid social position, confidence and deviousness.

There are different types of prose, in terms of register and complexity of syntax, and this plays a role in the delineation of character. A formal register used in an intimate situation, as in Act III scene 1, is often an indication that characters wish to distance themselves from their own actions, or else to justify them. Colloquial diction in an official setting is equally odd and in need of comment, as with Lucio's utterances during the final scene.

Language change

Four hundred years is a long time in the life of a language, so it is hardly surprising that we find differences between the language of a Shakespeare play and that of today. The 'rules' of modern English spelling, punctuation, grammar and syntax were not really established until the eighteenth century, and in Shakespeare's time language was much more flexible — we even find him inventing new words, **neologisms**, or using existing ones in a context in which no one had used them before. Frequently we find evidence of a language in flux, with archaic and modern usages working side by side.

There will obviously be some words in a Shakespearean text which are no longer current in modern English, or others, such as 'punk' (meaning prostitute), which are still used but not in the same way. There are also words that appear familiar but have changed their meaning, such as 'still' and 'presently' (which mean 'always' and 'now' respectively), and false friends that seem to be easily understood but are misleading, such as 'quit' (which meant to requite or to get your own back in Elizabethan English). 'You' is either a plural or an indication of respect to someone of higher authority, whereas 'thou', singular, suggests familiarity or affection, or talking down to a social inferior. This meant that it could be used as an insult or to suggest an irregular intimacy, and, conversely, using 'you' to a family member would convey coldness and a hostile relationship.

Verb forms were in the process of change in Shakespeare's time, so that you can find both the archaic forms of 'hath', wilt', 'canst' and so on for second and third person, as well as their modern equivalents. There is less use than nowadays of the auxiliary verb 'do' to express a negative or question and you are more likely to find 'knows he?' and 'he knows not' rather than 'does he know?' or 'he doesn't know'. Some past participles have changed, as in 'have forgot', 'have spoke', and subjects and verbs do not always agree, so that you can find singular subjects with plural verbs and vice versa, as well as verbs and nouns being used as interchangeable parts of speech. Word order was more flexible for Shakespeare, and the object could precede the verb for reasons of emphasis or metre. Conditionals were often formed without use of the word 'if', which could also be substituted by the word 'an', short for 'and'. Double negatives could be used for emphasis, such as 'nor nothing', as could double superlatives, as in 'most noblest', and 'nor…nor ' was more often used than 'neither…nor'.

None of these differences should interfere with an understanding of the meaning or be a barrier to appreciation. When we listen to the plays spoken by skilful actors, we understand things which seemed obscure on the page. Shakespeare's language, among other things, is poetry, and we should accept it as such. In responding to poetry, we are required to open our own imaginations to the mysterious power of words to make us see things afresh, from an unlikely angle or a startling perspective. Understanding does not have to be limited to working out a literal meaning; it can be intuitive, imaginative or emotional.

Scene summaries and notes

Act I scene 1

The Duke hands over the government of Vienna, in the presence of Escalus, to his deputy Angelo, claiming an urgent need to leave the city.

The imagery of minting and of reproduction is introduced in the Duke's first speech with the words 'pregnant' (line 11) and 'figure' (line 16), initiating recurring imagery of the stamped coin, legitimate tender and counterfeiting. The fineness of gold and the genuineness of coins were at the time tested by a touchstone, a piece of stone which left a distinctive mark on the metal to be tried (see lines 48–49 where Angelo uses this metaphor of himself). Angelo's request for a test of his 'metal' to be carried out can be interpreted as either overconfidence or diffidence. The testing of reputations begins immediately with the Duke asking Escalus his opinion of Angelo; he receives a cautious and diplomatic answer.

Angelo is instructed to let 'Mortality and mercy in Vienna/Live in thy tongue and heart' (lines 44–45). 'Mortality' and 'mercy' are oppositions in the judicial process, which dispenses either life or death, but it appears that Angelo is being told to arrive at a balance between the two, according to merit, and to make sure his words match his feelings.

In Renaissance ethics, virtues must be shared and implemented, not hidden like lights under bushels, which would be seen as a sinful waste of gifts given by God for a purpose on earth (see the Bible parable of the talents).

The Duke speaks in the royal plural using 'we' for 'I' to convey his superior status. His reference to not wishing to stage himself to the eyes of the people is thought to allude to the alleged dislike of crowds of the new King James.

Act I scene 2

Mistress Overdone informs Lucio and other gentlemen that Claudio has been arrested for making Juliet pregnant, and Pompey tells her about the proclamation to pluck down the houses of ill repute in the suburbs of Vienna. Claudio meets Lucio on his way to prison, and asks him to persuade his sister Isabella to intercede for him.

Described by Quiller-Couch (*The New Shakespeare* introduction, p. xl) as a scene of 'dismal dirtiness', Act 1 scene 2 begins *in medias res* and in prose as a strong contrast to the previous scene. Note that the subject is still the perversion of law for personal purposes and the Ten Commandments, although the emphasis is now on contemporary politics. The key word 'grace' is introduced via the unlikely mouth of Lucio. Praying for war as being more lucrative than peace is an example of moral perversion, and is followed by reference to venereal disease, a punishment for the unchaste.

Lucio tells us that Claudio 'was ever precise in promise-keeping', presumably giving testimony not only to his punctuality but to his ability to keep an oath and therefore his intention to marry Juliet. The prisoner passing over the stage is another victim of the new law, first to show it taking general effect, and also demonstrating how common the crime of 'groping for trouts in a peculiar river' is.

Although they are friends, the difference in social and moral status between Claudio and Lucio is marked by Lucio's preference for prose. Claudio's speech, beginning at line 156, is one long sentence of 16 lines, which reveals his agitation by the many parentheses, qualifications and **anacoluthons**, and quick changes of imagery – from horses to armour to zodiacs – and a high degree of 'compaction'. As Kermode points out, the use of 'prone' (line 182) (which baffled Dr Johnson) demonstrates Empson's seventh type of ambiguity, whereby 'the two meanings of the word [...] are the two opposite meanings defined by the context, so that the total effect is to show a fundamental division in the author's mind' (Empson, quoted in Kermode, p. 151). 'Prone' means either passive and immobile, lying flat and face downwards, or actively tending towards, as in 'she is prone to…'. This contradiction reflects the relevant **oxymoronic** concepts of a sexually provocative nun or a silent advocate. Critics have also pointed out the irony of Claudio's describing the effect Isabella is able to have on men in the sexual language of 'prone', 'move' and 'play'. There is a question of whether the tone of Claudio's comment is contrite resignation or sarcastic bitterness: 'On whom it will, it will;/On whom it will not, so; yet still 'tis just' (lines 121–22).

Act I scene 3

The Duke confides in Friar Thomas that he has handed over power to Angelo in order that the dormant laws should be enforced. He announces his intention to disguise himself as a friar.

The Duke **hubristically** declares himself immune from Cupid's dart. There is some incon-sistency in his explanation for his removal, allegedly to Poland. On the one hand, he wants the laws enforced which he has let slip for 14 years, and has therefore chosen a 'man of stricture and firm abstinence' (line 12) to do it; but on the other, he gives the impression at the end of the scene that Angelo is a 'seemer' and is not therefore the right man for the job. Perhaps he does not yet know that Angelo will fall (but see Act III scene 1) and is testing Puritanism generally.

Act I scene 4

Lucio tells Isabella what has befallen her brother. He persuades her to go to Angelo to plead for Claudio's life.

The opening portrays Isabella as extreme and wishing for more penitential restraints even than a nunnery demands. Lucio's behaviour in this scene is often questioned. In addition to his love of the sound of his own voice and his playing with language through its registers (what Kermode calls 'linguistic oscillation', p. 156), his speeches here seem to suggest an **ambivalence** in his view of women, or at least of Isabella. There is flattery, teasing and irreverence, but also a reluctant admiration which would parallel the effect she has on Angelo, and that which Eve had on Satan, who was impressed despite himself. Note that he addresses her in verse not prose. She believes that he is mocking her as a 'thing enskied and sainted' (line 34), and that he is therefore guilty of blasphemy.

The abundance of pregnancy and harvesting imagery in this scene implies that repro-duction is a natural process and therefore cannot be stopped by laws, or vows of chastity. Note Isabella's plea that Claudio should marry Juliet, as though marriage, ordained by God, is the cure for libertinism (a view expressed by St Paul, who said ''Tis better to marry than to burn', meaning to go to hell) and which gives a preview of the ending of the play. She does not, however, seem to be shocked by her brother's licentious behaviour, and this should be borne in mind when forming a view of her character, which is not simply that of a prude. Note that a beautiful woman who speaks to a man is considered dangerous (lines 12–13), and this prepares the audience for the outcome of the encounter between Isabella and Angelo.

Act II scene 1

Angelo is adamant to Escalus that Claudio must die. Elbow brings in Froth and Pompey and tells a tedious tale of pregnancy and prunes.

We see the contrast of attitude towards fallen men between the magistrate Escalus and the 'strict deputy' (I.2.180). Escalus is capable of feeling sympathy, even though he does not recommend mercy in this case ('Pardon is still the nurse of second woe./But yet, poor Claudio', lines 271–72). Bringing in lower and more gross libertines has the effect of suggesting that the lowlife of Vienna do indeed need disciplining, but also that Claudio's offence is much less rank than theirs and that Angelo has failed to make a necessary distinction. The scene contains the proleptic irony of Angelo saying that he would deserve the same punishment as Claudio should he similarly offend.

Elbow's **malapropistic** account and Pompey's verbal diarrhoea – **symbolic** of his sexual lack of control – is a parody of a trial. Pompey takes the role of judge, Froth is the accused and Elbow is the plaintiff, but each of them is unfit for his role, as Pompey is satirical, Froth incapable and Elbow farcical. Once again pregnancy and pre-marital sex is the topic. The character called Justice, who has only these ten words in total, is not the least of the strangenesses of the play. Critics have seen his utterances as pregnant with meaning, with a reference to the eleventh hour (the proximity of Juliet's delivery and Claudio's execution) and an *ex cathedra* condemnation: 'Lord Angelo is severe' (line 269).

Act II scene 2

The Provost pleads in vain with Angelo for Claudio's life. Lucio conducts Isabella into Angelo's presence and exhorts her to enter into a spirited and spiritual debate. She is told to return the next morning. Angelo reveals in private that he desires Isabella.

This is a set-piece debate between Mercy and Justice, described by the *Arden* editor as a 'terrible encounter of absolutes' (introduction, p. lxix). Isabella argues that her brother is 'not prepared for death' (line 84, later used as the reason to reprieve Barnardine) and that therefore his execution would be murder. It is ironic and presumably significant that Isabella plants the idea of a bribe in Angelo's head (and worries Lucio) in line 145. One must remember that virtuous women were not available for sexual purposes at this time, and her habit makes her even less accessible: Isabella constitutes forbidden fruit for Angelo, who commits the sin of Adam by putting concupiscence before secular and spiritual duty. Paradoxically it brings him to life, replacing the 'snow-broth' (I.4.58) in his veins with hot blood, while he directs others towards spiritual or actual death. The number of **asides** in this scene, uttered by Provost, Lucio and Angelo, conveys the tension of the situation and the impression that Isabella, while the focus of the attention of three males, is naively unaware of the effect and significance of her presence and speech.

Act II scene 3

The disguised Duke visits the prison and talks to the Provost and Juliet, who is repentant but insists that both the love and the fault are mutual between herself and Claudio.

Adopting a disguise was a form of symbolic death in the theatre of the time, and the convention was that despite the easy recognisability of voices and body movements, disguise was always impenetrable even by spouses and close relatives. Imagery of weight and heaviness is used in this scene, representing the burdens of pregnancy and transgression. A pregnant woman was not physically punished in Shakespeare's time (traditionally a female criminal could plead her belly and be let off), but her seducer often was.

On the other hand, the woman's reputation was destroyed (she 'blistered her report', line 12), while the man's, if anything, was enhanced ('fit to do another such offence', line 14). This is the only scene in which Juliet speaks, and it is to rebel against the notion that the sexes should be treated unequally for a mutual act.

Act II scene 4

Isabella returns to Angelo and, after much theological debate, is told that her brother will be spared if she will give up her virginity to Angelo. Isabella feels she has no choice but to let her brother die.

This dialogue has many shared lines, which show similarity of mind and the sparring of intellectual equals, and which ironically create an intimacy between characters who can predict each other's thoughts well enough to finish each other's lines. Angelo's **soliloquy** reveals a soul in torment; like Claudius in *Hamlet* he is torn between guilt and desire. He admits that outward forms of piety and authority can mislead the onlooker, and that devils and angels are interchangeable. It is casuistical of Angelo to claim, using coining imagery, that conceiving an illegitimate child is as bad a crime as murder.

Isabella is adamant that what matters is her soul and not her body; she believes that she cannot accede to Angelo's physical demand without incurring damnation – as a novice nun she is required to believe this – even though he argues that it would be an act of charity and therefore not a sin. Isabella insists that 'Better it were a brother died at once/Than that a sister, by redeeming him,/Should die for ever' (lines 106–07) and that 'lawful mercy is/Nothing kin to foul redemption' (lines 112–13). Unlike the Duke, she does not subscribe to the view that the end justifies the means. She is, in any case, right not to trust that Angelo would keep his part of the bargain and free her brother. Women had no public voice or credibility, and Angelo reminds her that because he is male and of high rank, no one would listen if she were to try to expose him. The image of scales is used to make it clear that he weighs more heavily, and Isabella's soliloquy reveals her weighing her brother's life against her chastity and finding him lighter.

Act III scene 1

The Duke, as prison priest, prepares Claudio for death. Isabella tells Claudio that it is better he should die than that she should lose her honour. The Duke forms a plot to substitute Isabella for Mariana in a sexual encounter with Angelo, and Isabella agrees to it.

This scene, in which the Duke becomes the ***deus ex machina*** who has to resolve the impasse involving Angelo, Claudio and Isabella, is generally reckoned to contain the best poetry of the play. The Duke's long opening speech is a standard medieval consolation speech (as used by Boethius); Claudio's moving and metaphorical speech on death, however, has been compared to Hamlet's famous 'To be or not to be' soliloquy, and is distinctly Renaissance in tone. Pater (quoted in Palmer, p. 60) thought 'perhaps the most eloquent of all Shakespeare's words' are given here to Claudio. His contemplation of the afterlife laments its trials – stressed by the three words ending in '-less': 'viewless', 'restless', 'lawless' – of blindness, perpetual motion, and chaos. The emphasis is on coldness and lack of feeling, as typified by the icy Angelo. There is a textual problem with the word 'delighted' (line 124) which Kermode suggests should be read 'de-lighted'.

Claudio is at first persuaded to embrace death, but reaffirms his desire to live after Isabella's arrival, her somewhat tactless urging of him to get ready to die tomorrow, and her explanation of the deal which the 'outward-sainted deputy' (line 92) is offering. It seems she only expects Claudio to live for another 'six or seven winters' anyway (line 79), which is perhaps her self-deceiving justification for alleging that her honour matters more than his continuing existence. She also suggests that she thinks he is too cowardly to die. These gambits can be seen as either desperation, immaturity, callousness or disingenuity, hence the debate which rages over how we should interpret Isabella. It could be said that for Claudio to gain his life through Isabella's degradation is similar to Pompey's role of profiting from the sale of female bodies for sex, and that this would make Claudio a pimp. Line 154 is the last spoken by Isabella to Claudio in the play: ''Tis best that thou diest quickly.' She says the same of Mariana in line 233, in her youth not recognising, or in her zealousness not accepting, the absoluteness of death.

It is unaccountable that suddenly, at line 150, the Duke and Isabella should drop into prose, and not grand prose at that. As Quiller-Couch puts it categorically (*The New Shakespeare* introduction, p. xxxix): 'The two halves of this scene cannot be made of a piece by anyone possessing even a rudimentary acquaintance with English prose and poetry.' Critics are generally agreed that the quality of the writing – the tenseness and evocativeness of the imagery – undergoes an abrupt and irrecoverable change from this point onwards in the play.

It is ironic that God's deputy in a friar's outfit and a novice nun in her habit should arrange the bed trick. The Duke/friar also lies to Claudio, both about Angelo's intentions in assaying Isabella's virtue and about the inevitability of Claudio's impending death. By revealing the story of Mariana and the loss of her dowry, and by referring to the suitor who rejected her as 'this well-seeming Angelo' (lines 224–25), the Duke is also admitting that he has known about Angelo's true, cold and materialistic nature ('a marble to her tears' and guilty of 'unjust unkindness') since before the beginning of the play, which calls into question his real motives for making him his 'substitute'. The play then becomes the unmasking of Angelo for reasons already proven, rather than a testing of Angelo and his falling for the first time because of being unable to withstand temptation. It is the breaking of his vows to Mariana and the damaging of her reputation – making him no better than Lucio – which have caused the need for him to be 'scaled' (line 255), rather than his refusal to accept a wife without a dowry (which was a common enough position at the time and until much later). As critics gleefully point out, Isabella is able not only to tolerate but also to facilitate Mariana's committing the same act – with potentially the same outcome – as Juliet committed, and to agree to another virgin female undergoing the same experience which she has refused for herself as being not only sinful but a fate worse than death. However, Isabella believes she is being given this advice by a man of God and pre-marital contracts had legal recognition.

Act III scene 2

Pompey goes to prison for procuring; Lucio refuses to stand bail for him and then slanders the Duke unwittingly but persistently to his face, believing him to be a friar. Mistress Overdone goes to prison for prostitution. The Duke has a conversation with Escalus about both Claudio's sentence and Angelo.

Pompey is the living example of what happens if there is too much leniency, which must be distinguished from mercy; the latter is active not passive, and should be applied sparingly and justifiably. The Duke calls him a 'rude beast' (line 31), which prepares us for the entry, or non-entry, of Barnardine. The exchange between Lucio and the Duke is comic, but the crime of destroying a reputation by slander (a kind of false creation or murder) is a serious one, for which Lucio will be sentenced later. It is perhaps significant that he refuses to help a friend in need, a 'brother' who calls upon him – unlike Isabella later.

Later on in the scene, Lucio refuses to acknowledge that he is a father. Thus another illegitimate coining is revealed and laid at Lucio's door, testimony to the laxity of the Duke's regime and providing another case of a woman promised marriage and then abandoned. Ironically, in saying how much he preferred the Duke in power – since he 'would have dark deeds darkly answered' (lines 166–67), compared to 'this ungenitured agent' (line 164) Angelo – Lucio considers that he is praising the Duke. Escalus, deceived by the Duke's disguise, praises him for his moderation as 'a gentleman of all temperance' (line 227). The 11 couplets the Duke delivers to close the act are a sententious set piece and give the impression that he is playing the role of an impersonal **choric** figure. Being in octosyllabic verse they invite comment/comparison with the epilogue to *The Tempest*, spoken by Duke Prospero.

Act IV scene 1

Mariana the recluse receives the Duke in the moated grange. Isabella arrives and tells the Duke about the arrangements for meeting Angelo. Isabella gets Mariana to agree to the 'bed-trick'.

This is a familiar scene from the play, popularised by Tennyson's poems 'Mariana' and 'The Lady of Shalott'. The disrupted boy's song is considered 'one of the loveliest songs of Shakespeare' (Pater quoted in Palmer, p. 57). It seems odd that the Duke is 'a man of comfort' (line 8) who has often given her solace, since he has only just become a friar, as far as the audience is aware, yet Mariana tells him that she is 'always bound to you' (line 24). It is also odd that the Duke switches from verse to prose mid-speech at line 16.

The garden with a locked gate to which someone has acquired the key is the medieval symbol of an assault on female chastity (still being used by Jane Austen in *Mansfield Park* in the early nineteenth century). Note the Shakespeare coinage 'circummured' (line 27) meaning 'walled round'. Mariana is in effect imprisoned until her reputation is salvaged. The 'heavy middle of the night' (line 34) is an interesting phrase (and one which fascinated Keats), which contributes to the imagery of weight in the play.

The Isabella of this scene, full of practical advice and devious action, seems to be a very different Isabella from the one full of moral precepts. There is also a structural problem in that the time allowed for Isabella to persuade Mariana, a complete stranger, occupies only six lines of the Duke's blank verse and even these few stop-gap lines seem to have been misplaced and to belong to the Duke's previous speech (III.2.175–78). Line 71 refers to the 'pre-contract' between Angelo and Mariana which, though less binding than that of Claudio and Juliet, could not be dissolved without the consent of both parties and would become a common-law marriage in the event of consummation. The matter of pre-nuptial contracts is a complicated issue about which commentators seem confused. The fullest account is given in the *Arden* introduction (pp. liii–v), which contradicts the version given in the Penguin commentary (p. 173) on this scene.

Act IV scene 2

The Provost recruits Pompey as helper to Abhorson, the executioner. Claudio is shown his death warrant. The Duke arrives to say there is hope for his reprieve, but Angelo's messenger brings a note to say that Claudio is to be beheaded, and even sooner than planned, and that his head is to be sent as proof to Angelo. The Duke finally persuades the Provost to kill another prisoner, Barnardine, instead.

It is an ironic reversal, which equates the two practices, that Pompey is now to take life away when he has been instrumental in the creating of it. As the Duke says, Pompey and the executioner 'weigh equally' (line 27). Abhorson's name is presumably a moral naming like those of the other low characters (see the list at the beginning of Act IV scene 3 in addition to those in the cast list) referring to abortion, or the idea of an abhorred son, or the son of a whore, all of which would be relevant. The Provost calls attention to the anomaly of Claudio and Barnardine having received the same sentence of capital punishment, though their offences are opposite. This is the scene in which the night references give way to those of dawn, as if it is here that the dark play reveals itself as an intending comedy, despite the 'bitter deputy' (line 75). Barnardine here fails the humanity test, one of many tests in the play; the Provost is then given another. The production of a ring to prove identity and authority and with the power of life or death is a fairytale plot device, like disguise and substitution. That the executioner used to ask for forgiveness from a felon before taking his life highlights the supposed difference between unjust murder and just execution, and the religious importance of being forgiven. The prose conversation between the Duke and the Provost is surprising, given their status; that Friars would have spoken in verse is not only shown in other plays (see *Romeo and Juliet*) but elsewhere within this play (see end of Act IV). The Duke has taken on a conjurer's powers similar to those of Prospero in *The Tempest*, and he speaks a similar line: 'Put not yourself into amazement how these things should be' (lines 197–98).

Act IV scene 3

Barnardine proves unfit for execution so the Provost offers to substitute and send to Angelo the head of a pirate already dead, one Ragozine. The Duke tells Isabella that Claudio is dead, and that the Duke will return that evening. He gives her a letter for Friar Peter, who will take on her own and Mariana's cause against Angelo.

Commentators have been unable to account for Barnardine's existence at all in the play, since he refuses his only role, which is to die, and Ragozine performs the plot device adequately. Lascelles (pp. 70–71) says Barnardine is 'the man who will always [...] make constituted authority appear ridiculous'. 'I swear I will not die today for any man's persuasion' (line 58) is a clear statement of resistance to the very concept of the law, and as such he is Claudio's opposite. Rossiter considers that: 'In this world of tottering values and disordered will, Barnardine stands out as admirable.' However, he is shown to have fallen below human status on the chain of being. He is a beast, living in straw like an animal, constantly drunk or asleep, and therefore incapable of reason, unwilling to accept judgement, oblivious to morality, 'insensible of mortality' (IV.2.141). It exercised Shakespeare's contemporaries to know how to treat such threatening non-human specimens of humanity, 'Unfit to live or die' (line 62). The right to be prepared for one's passage into the afterlife was an important matter of faith for the Elizabethans. The Duke is proved fallible in this scene; his failure with Barnardine is similar to Prospero's inability to make Caliban fall into line in *The Tempest*. Evil cannot be made to obey the designs of the good and refuses to observe the restraints of agreed social and religious codes of conduct. It requires 'an accident that heaven provides' (line 75) to enforce human justice on earth (the conclusion Hamlet also arrives at).

The Duke has been criticised for prolonging Isabella's suffering in not telling her that Claudio is alive, and it may seem harsh to a modern audience, but there is religious precedent for this as another form of testing (cf. Job) whereby someone can prove their worth only under duress (a point Angelo makes at the beginning, and which mirrors Alonso's trial in *The Tempest*, where Prospero continues to let him believe that his son is dead until his repentance has been secured). Isabella proves her 'patience' (line 117) after an initial angry outburst; she accepts heaven's ordinance, personified by the friar, in her utterance 'I am directed by you' (line 135).

As the *Arden* editor points out (note, p. 116) there is evidence of hasty revision and careless rewriting of this scene in the form of various anomalies and ambiguities towards the end of it: morning changes to evening; Lucio returns instead of the Provost; there is confusion about who is being referred to as 'him' in line 95, and why Varrius needs to be involved at all. Mention of a 'consecrated fount' (line 96) is a reminder of the religious significance of the role of the Duke and the judgement of Angelo. 'By cold gradation' (line 98) has given editors difficulty, but presumably means 'through dispassionate measured process', thus reinforcing the main image and theme of the play.

Act IV scene 4

Angelo discusses with Escalus the Duke's imminent return, which he is worried by. He then admits when alone to a sense of regret for Claudio's supposed death and his own fall from grace.

The mixture of prose and verse used by Angelo indicates his perturbed state of mind and is evidence of his split personality as saint and devil. His later rehabilitation is prefigured by his twice expressing regret in his soliloquy for having, as he thinks, executed Claudio, and audiences, enjoying the **dramatic irony**, find him at his most sympathetic during this speech. This is the first of three extremely short scenes, which give the impression that time is about to catch up with Angelo. His mention of the devil is followed by a knock, as if he has summoned him, a common belief at the time. That Isabella is at the door is an ironic juxtaposition which reinforces the paradoxical idea that she is the devil in disguise, at least as far as Angelo is concerned.

Act IV scene 5

The Duke is himself again. He instructs Friar Peter about the arrangements for his public return to the city, and greets Varrius.

These two very short scenes achieve the purpose of creating tension around the impending return of the Duke and trial of Angelo. It becomes clear that a large gathering will be present as an audience and that the Duke will have directed his friends and officers in their role, down to having scripted the lines and stage directions for his 'players', and now seems confidently in control of the situation and impending drama. In medieval times all the handing over of ownership of cities took place at the main city gate, so the location is symbolic.

Act IV scene 6

Isabella tells Mariana that the Duke has instructed her to confront and accuse Angelo, and that she is uneasy about having been given this part. Friar Peter comes to conduct them to a position of vantage in the crowd to welcome the Duke back.

The audience is prepared for the fact that the Duke may play devil's advocate (***advocatus diaboli***) and appear to be against Isabella during the trial. The sounding of trumpets gives a suitably ceremonious and grave air to the occasion, reminding the audience that the Day of Judgement shall be thus heralded.

Act V scene 1

The Duke appears with followers and greets Angelo. Isabella demands justice. Friar Peter brings Isabella to the Duke and she accuses Angelo. The Duke at first pretends to believe that she is mad. Lucio speaks up for her, but is silenced by the Duke. The Duke asks to see Friar Lodowick (i.e. himself) and when he cannot be produced as a witness Isabella is led away to prison. Mariana tells the Duke she is Angelo's wife, but he denies it. The Duke leaves Escalus in charge and goes to disguise himself again. Escalus is about to arrest him for slander to the state when he reveals himself. Angelo is ordered to marry Mariana. Angelo is condemned to death. Mariana and the returned Isabella plead for him. Barnardine is released. Claudio is revealed as alive. Angelo is acquitted. Lucio is ordered to marry Kate Keepdown, the prostitute he made pregnant, which he claims is a worse punishment than whipping or hanging. As a parting shot the Duke announces his intention to marry Isabella, who is given no chance to either agree or disagree.

This is an exceptionally long scene/act, similar to that at the end of *The Tempest* in which harmony is restored, somewhat forcibly, by the ruler. This scene, which takes the whole act, is the dénouement in that disguises actual and metaphorical are thrown off, and the truth is revealed and recognised. It is also the Day of Judgement for everyone except the Duke (who is the judge), but re-birth follows death, as a Christian allegory, since marriage is a hopeful beginning and Angelo is re-minted as a 'new-married man' (line 397).

True to the constraints of Shakespearean drama all remaining characters are required to attend, so even Barnardine has to be fetched. The Duke's entrance with a retinue makes clear that he has assumed the status we have not seen him exercise before, as a reinvented public presence and law-giver to the populace. A prison image is used in line 10, making it clear that everything will now be unlocked and exposed to public gaze and the light of day. The language of this scene is formal and stylised, as befits a trial scene, with much use of repetition, triple syntactical structures (e.g. lines 32 and 38–41) and rhetorical questions and exclamations. The Duke says of Lucio 'Silence that fellow' (line 181) and Escalus of the Duke (as Lodowick) 'Let him speak no more' (lines 343–44), recreating the courtroom practice of controlling utterance.

The Duke refers to Angelo as his 'cousin' three times (lines 1, 165 and 252). This is the first suggestion that there is kinship between the two, though it would be usual to delegate authority to a relative at this time. If so, this adds another dimension to the situation and their relationship. Critics disagree over whether the Duke's treatment of Lucio is vindictive or generous; bear in mind he now commits a double slander on the Duke by calling Friar Lodowick a 'meddling', 'saucy' and 'scurvy' friar who spoke against the Duke. It seems odd to some critics (see Quiller-Couch, p. xl) that the Duke should give so much attention to Lucio in the finale while the two who count most – Isabella and Claudio – stand silent in the background. However, Lucio is a murderer of reputations, which was a serious felony in the period and one James I felt particularly strongly about.

Mercy was seen, and often personified, as a feminine attribute and balance to male aggression, as in medieval tournaments where the winning knight would ask his mistress to indicate whether or not his opponent's life should be spared (and see Portia's famous speech in *The Merchant of Venice* on the 'quality of mercy'). Isabella has to give a false statement, that she lost her virginity to Angelo, in order 'To make the truth appear where it seems hid' (line 66). Mariana's refusal to show her face is both a dramatic requirement, a continuation of the disguise theme (there are three disguised characters in this scene), and a reminder of women's subservience to their husbands. There is no social role for a woman who is neither 'maid, widow nor wife' and therefore Mariana is defined either as 'nothing' (line 178) or as a prostitute ('punk', line 519). Angelo reinforces this impression of their lowly status by assuming some man must be behind the women's allegations, not believing them capable of independent action.

Angelo allies himself to Lucio, shown in lines 322 and 347, perhaps recognising a kindred proud spirit. Quiller-Couch argues (*The New Shakespeare* introduction, p. xlii) that it is hard to take this scene seriously because Lucio turns it into comedy in spite of itself and undermines the solemnity of the occasion by refusing to recognise authority and usurping the role of the Duke. This is demonstrated by his insistence on speaking prose when all about him are speaking verse, and by his continuing to play the fool even in his own extremity. Revealingly, Lucio cannot be silenced and continues to challenge the Duke to the very end of the play.

The Duke's capitulation to the 'dribbling dart of love' is a traditional comedic nod to the power of Cupid. It is also acceptance of the Pauline doctrine that 'It is better to marry than to burn', i.e. than to go to hell for sexual activity outside wedlock. Isabella not only pleads for mercy for Angelo, as an act of charity on behalf of Mariana, but argues for a mitigation of Angelo's offence on the morally dubious but legally accepted grounds that he did not do the thing for which he is being sentenced to death, but only intended it. She is bearing her belief in Claudio's death in a Job-like Christian manner. She has nothing further to gain or lose at this point, therefore her charity is clearly proven.

There is still a remnant of pride in Angelo, since he 'entreats' (line 474) death rather than face the shame that mercy would bring him; or perhaps he is still being 'precise' and knows his life is forfeit to the law. It seems irrational that Barnardine, the actual murderer, should be let off scot-free. Perhaps this is because he is the one man without a mask whereas all the rest have been doubters and seemers, or to demonstrate the arbitrary aspect of the administration of justice, or as an admission that sometimes justice cannot be applied and an 'apt remission' (line 495) is more appropriate, or to comment that rough justice is the best humans can manage. The most likely reason is to enact the philosophy, expressed later by Pope, that 'To err is human, to forgive divine'.

Plot

There are eight specified locations in the play: ducal palace, public street, friar's cell, courtroom, prison, nunnery, moated grange and city gate. The majority of them are prisons of one kind or another, with gates and boundaries and restrictions on who may enter or leave. The places can also be categorised by gender and class, creating the effect of a segregated city; Lucio is as out of place in the nunnery as Froth is in the brothel and Juliet is in prison.

A number of features of the plot are reflected across the three different social levels. Higher and lower orders committing the same deeds provides a source of irony in many of Shakespeare's comedies and tragedies. In this play, Claudio the 'gentleman' considers selling his sister's body for his own profit, which makes him no better than Pompey the pimp. Claudio has also impregnated Juliet, which puts him in danger of being considered on the same level as Lucio, a known fornicator. When Angelo loses patience with the comic trial of Froth and walks out, leaving Escalus in charge, there is an echo of the Duke's act of delegation and preference for more serious matters. The Duke's infatuation with Isabella, despite previously claiming he would never marry (being immune to 'the dribbling dart of love', I.3.2), is strangely similar to Angelo's in that they are attracted by her innocence, which Lucio also seems to feel. Lucio slanders the Duke to anyone who will listen; the Duke also has criticisms to make about Angelo behind his back, though he flatters him to his face. Like Angelo, Elbow and Barnardine (in different ways) both make a mockery of the law by showing how difficult it is to apply. Elbow's arrest of Froth parallels Angelo's arrest of Claudio, and Elbow thinks he is being accused of pre-marital cohabitation with his own wife. Mariana's rejection by Angelo parallels that of Kate Keepdown by the other oath-breaker, Lucio. Claudius and Barnardine share a reluctance to be executed. Like Barnardine, Lucio undermines the solemnity of the judgement ritual by refusing to recognise the judge's authority; they are equally resistant to being educated, being selfish and sensual beings not receptive to reason.

A feature of the plot of *Measure for Measure* is its dependence on events which happened prior to the beginning of the play: Angelo's rejection of Mariana; Claudio's proposal to and impregnation of Juliet; the Duke's realisation that Vienna is going to the dogs and his decision to test Angelo; Lucio's rejection of Kate; Isabella's decision to become a nun. The audience thus feels that it is seeing a set of consequences of earlier decisions or transgressions being fulfilled. On the other hand, in contrast to other plays, there are no missing scenes once the play begins, no meetings between characters which are reported but which the audience does not see. This gives the impression of laying everything bare, as in a courtroom, with all hiding places and retreats, actual and metaphorical, now exposed.

The plot could also be described as consisting primarily of non-action and non-event in that very little actually happens in the play, in terms of plans being put into effect, compared to what fails to happen. The Duke does not really carry out his declared intention to be absent, nor his intention to remain celibate. Angelo's engagement was an inconclusive plan, as was Isabella's intention to become a nun. Mariana, on her own, does not nor could not succeed in winning back Angelo, given her withdrawal from the city, and nor could Mistress Overdone and Kate persuade Lucio to do the decent thing. Even Barnardine refuses to be executed according to plan. Isabella is unable to succeed in persuading Angelo, as he is unable to succeed in seducing her; nor does he keep his promise to spare Claudio. Claudio, on his own, does not find a way to save himself nor to marry Juliet. It is only through the ***deus ex machina*** intervention of the Duke that wrongs are righted and situations are changed, though these proclaimed solutions and sentences do not all take place on stage. Perhaps we are to interpret this as a play of ideas rather than of actions — confirmed by the large number of dilemmas faced by characters and abstractions used in the language of the play. Alternatively, perhaps we are being shown, as in *Hamlet*, how it is presumptuous of humans to make any plans at all, as only heaven (represented by the Duke) can 'direct us' and decide what will be.

Bed and head tricks

The head trick and the bed trick have been found morally unacceptable or objectionable by many critics and audiences. There is a long tradition in drama and fiction of substitutions to resolve dilemmas and stalemates. The morality of such tricks may seem dubious to a modern audience, but would not have caused concern at the time. On the contrary, such sleights of hand were admired as a clever and practical way of putting things right — the end justifies the means: ''tis a physic/That's bitter to sweet end' (IV.6.7–8), 'Th'offence pardons itself' (V.1.531). Like Chaucer, Shakespeare makes use of the swapping of persons or parts of their anatomy in many of his comedies, some of which rely on a substitute twin for their resolutions as well as their comic effects, as in *Twelfth Night* and *The Comedy of Errors*. Substitutions are only one step away from disguise, another way of exchanging one thing or person for another, which the Duke is practising when he becomes Friar Lodowick. This idea is an extension of the romance device of the king who roams freely disguised as a beggar, and of the necessity for a woman to dress as a man in order to be able to have a public role, like Portia in *The Merchant of Venice*.

The bed (or maidenhead) trick comes from Boccaccio (see *Arden* introduction, p. liii) and is also used, perhaps with better excuse, in *All's Well That Ends Well*. In both cases, the substitute is a woman suspected of being 'of easy virtue'. In *Measure for Measure* the saving of one girl's honour at the expense of another's is more equivocal, but nonetheless it is indubitably of double benefit. It is very much in Mariana's interests as well as Isabella's to agree to the swap; the only way she could ever be rescued from incarceration and social ostracism is to become Angelo's wife by fulfilling the nuptial agreement through consummation.

The head trick seems somewhat more distasteful, but since the audience has not met the 'most notorious pirate', and he is condemned to die anyway, it is difficult to fault the logic of 'The head of Ragozine for Claudio's'. It is perhaps worth noting, however, that the Captain in *Twelfth Night* is also considered by Illyrians to be a 'notable pirate', but his execution would have seriously damaged the comic mode of that play. In addition, the production of a severed head on stage is a feature of *Macbeth* and more appropriate to tragedy generally.

Marriage as reward and punishment

Many commentators and students find the marriage pairings, the conduct of the Duke, and Isabella's failure to respond to the Duke's proposal as obstacles to their whole-hearted endorsement of the play. Leavis says that ultimately 'what one makes of the ending [...] depends on what one makes of the Duke' (*Scrutiny* X, p. 243), and Rossiter agrees, concluding that we find the Duke ambiguous and that therefore the ending is ambiguous too (*Fifteen Lectures on Shakespeare,* p. 168). Rossiter claims that the Duke's characterisation does not match the Christian ethic dimension of the play; what ought to be does not match with what is, with the perceived experience of characters and audience, and therefore the play lacks conviction.

Of primary concern for critics and audiences is the use of marriage as a tool of punishment for Angelo, Lucio, and arguably Isabella, who all in their different ways have shown a lack of moderation. Some commentators have felt that the pairings are purely expedient and that the Duke should marry Mariana and Isabella should marry Angelo, on grounds of compatibility as well as following the source in the latter case. The paramount importance of a woman's reputation must have been a factor in Shakespeare deciding to give Mariana to Angelo. Perhaps he also felt that the Duke, as hero, deserved no less than the saintly and intelligent Isabella. Her failure to respond to his proposal has no obvious explanation. It may be a textual oversight; it may be, like Iago's refusal to speak at the end of *Othello*, a way of drawing attention to her shock at her purposes having been wrenched awry; it may be that there is nothing for her to say, since it is in fact a command not a request. But it makes it impossible to guess how she actually feels about the proposition, and leaves a loose end. Coleridge put on record his violent antipathy to the ending of the play:

> *Measure for Measure* is the single exception to the delightfulness of Shakespeare's plays. It is a hateful work, although Shakespearean throughout. Our feelings of justice are grossly wounded in Angelo's escape. Isabella herself contrives to be unamiable, and Claudio is detestable.
>
> [...] the pardon and marriage of Angelo not merely baffles the strong indignant claim of justice [...] but it is likewise degrading to the character of woman.

Characters

Dramatis personae

Duke Vincentio is ruler of Vienna. He is celibate, uninterested in marriage and devoted to his religious studies. He feels he has been too lax in his government of the city, which has fallen into immoral ways during a long period of neglect.

Angelo is deputy to Vincentio. He is a moral zealot and a Puritan. Up to now he has led an apparently blameless but controlled and restricted life. He was formerly betrothed to Mariana but broke off the engagement. His name can be viewed as ironic and is used as such in the play.

Escalus is an ancient lord. His unusual and symbolic name lends him a classical dignity and suggests measurement and balance. His views are moderate and sound, combining humanity and justice.

Claudio, the only brother of Isabella, is betrothed to the pregnant Juliet, whom he intends to marry. He is a conventional young man of the times, of the rank of 'gentleman' and the son of respectable parents, though he is known to Pompey and Mistress Overdone, and is a member of Lucio's circle. He is not an intellectual, and 'his reaction to his own plight oscillates between the extreme attitudes of the Duke's two deputies' (*Arden* introduction, p. lxvii).

Lucio is described in the *dramatis personae* as 'a Fantastic', meaning a libertine, 'a fellow of much licence', who epitomises irresponsibility and disrespect for authority, as evidenced by his slandering of the Duke. His being greeted as a friend by both Claudio and Pompey makes him a social go-between. He has a year-old child, by a prostitute called Kate Keepdown, whom he has not acknowledged. He likes to gossip and play go-between, giving himself dramatic importance. Like other licensed Fools in Shakespeare's plays, Lucio is no fool, and he makes valid comments on his rulers and their times.

Provost is the prison governor and is not given a name to individualise him.

Elbow is a simple constable and has held the post for seven and a half years, it being a job no one wants. He is officious in his duties and enjoys his powers to arrest others, including those above him in social status. His name makes him ridiculous.

Froth is a foolish gentleman with no intelligence and trivial interests, as his name implies. He frequents the underworld of the backstreets of Vienna looking for entertainment. Many of Shakespeare's comedies have such a character (e.g. Sir Andrew Aguecheek in *Twelfth Night*) to create satirical comedy and to provide moral comparison with serious characters.

Pompey is a tapster, a pimp, and servant to Mistress Overdone, with the unlikely but humorous surname of 'Bum'. He is sometimes also described in *dramatis personae* as a clown, which then meant uneducated member of the lower orders rather than a comedian, though Pompey is both. His name may be a play on 'puppy', putting him among the animal class and explaining the line in Act III

scene 2, 'Go to kennel, Pompey'. He is a barrack-room lawyer and resister of restraint, opposing laws on the grounds that they curb natural instinct (a view shared by Lucio). Like many of Shakespeare's tradesmen and petty criminals, he endears himself to the audience — which then contained more Pompeys than Dukes — with his satirical jibes.

Abhorson is an executioner, trained and employed by the state to carry out capital punishment by beheading or hanging. He is blunt of speech, and his name is indicative of his repellent profession, in which he trains Pompey.

Barnardine is a self-confessed murderer and drunkard who has been a prisoner in Vienna's jail for nine years. He is described as a 'dissolute prisoner', meaning he lives and behaves like an animal and has no remorse for his crime. He represents the depths to which humanity can sink, and is the product of the laws in Vienna having slept for so long.

Isabella is Claudio's sister and a novice nun. She wears a white habit as a member of the order of St Clare, an extreme sect of Catholicism. She has the moral passion and craving for absolutes of the idealistic adolescent. Her name means 'devoted to God' in Hebrew.

Mariana was betrothed five years previously to Angelo, who broke off the engagement when her dowry failed to materialise as a result of her brother Frederick's losses at sea. The reason he gave for breaking the nuptial contract was that her reputation was 'disvalued', as a result of which Mariana has had to spend the intervening time living outside of Viennese society in a secluded country grange, visited only by the Duke, apparently disguised as a friar. Perhaps her name suggests that she is cognate with the Virgin Mary, both wife and maid, and therefore has a redemptive role to play.

Juliet is on stage only three times and speaks only once. Her role is to be seen as obviously with child, and her muteness increases the **pathos** of her condition, which symbolises the consequences of sexual licentiousness.

Mistress Overdone is Pompey's employer and a bawd, i.e. a brothel keeper, and has been so for 11 years. Her name refers amusingly to the fact that she has had nine husbands. She reveals Lucio's secret of his illegitimate child by the prostitute Kate Keepdown, which she is looking after.

Vincentio: the duke of dark corners

Lucio calls the Duke 'the old fantastical duke of dark corners' (IV.3.155–56). There are many different ways of judging the judge in *Measure for Measure*, but his decision to absent himself from his position of upholder of the law of Vienna is problematical. There are many Shakespearean Dukes — for example in *Othello, Romeo and Juliet* and *A Midsummer Night's Dream* — and whether they are playing a role in a **tragedy** or **comedy**, they are notable for their ability to be fair and firm in their dealings with the public. The Elizabethans believed that *noblesse oblige*, i.e. that rank involved responsibility, and that abdication from the duty of applying the law and following the affairs of state would be followed by anarchy or usurpation. This is shown in the case of Prospero, the Duke of Milan in *The Tempest* who spent too much time in his study. Some critics see Duke Vincentio as a satirical portrait of James I, who shut himself away from his people in order to write his books, dismissing the populace as scandalmongers.

Although the Duke admits his failures as upholder and administrator of the law and allegedly believes that his deputy will make a better job of it, Kermode comments on the apparent mixed motives of the Duke: does he want Angelo to be successful and to enforce laws he cannot, or is he testing Angelo and expecting him to fail, already having doubts about his 'stricture and firm abstinence' (I.3.12)? A contemporary audience would have grave reservations — similar to those felt at the beginning of *King Lear* — about the Duke's fitness to rule and his wisdom in deciding to deputise his task, and might see him as a culpable figure who has failed to provide leadership and a good example, thereby causing the disorder which exists before and during the play.

Character or stereotype?

It has been argued that Duke Vincentio of Vienna 'undergoes no inner development of character and achieves no added self-knowledge' (*Arden* introduction, p. xcv), which supports the view that by virtue of his position he is not a real character. He is seen as less delineated and realised than any of the other four main characters. Muir, quoting Lawrence, calls him 'a stage Duke', a mere instrument in the play's economy' (p. 113), and Quiller-Couch denounces him as 'a stage-puppet…a wearisome man, talking rubbish' (*The New Shakespeare* introduction, p. xxxiii).

Like the stock literary character, the fairytale prince, the Duke uses disguise to slip out of his palace at night and mingle with his subjects to better know and understand them, before returning to his rightful position in the morning. On the other hand, by proposing to Isabella he, like her, is renouncing 'the life removed' (I.3.8) and joining the human race, and his exchanges with Lucio in particular show a sense of personality and even humour. His inability to make things happen at the time and in the manner he would wish is evidence of a flawed human being rather than a perfect one. He could also be said to be guilty of **hubris** when he claims to be above nature in being immune to 'the dribbling dart of love' (I.3.2). His ironic punishment by the gods makes him more than just a stereotypical Duke and different from Duke Escalus in *Romeo and Juliet* for instance, or even Duke Theseus in *A Midsummer Night's Dream*, who maintains his superhuman status throughout.

Duke as Providence

The Duke's dramatic function is to lead the other characters through chaos back to a restoration of order and the regeneration of legitimate offspring. Leavis calls him 'Peripatetic Providence' and other critics have gone so far as to suggest that, like Christ, he left and came again in order that souls might be saved. Like God, 'Duke Vincentio moves in a mysterious way' (Rossiter, p. 168). As head of church and state, he is responsible for his flock, a shepherd called up by 'th'unfolding star' (IV.2.196). His dressing as a friar would have been seen by a contemporary audience as symbolic of his divine status, as well as being a necessary device for allowing him private access to unmarried women. True virtue and 'the demigod Authority' (I.2.119) are invested in him (as they are in Prospero, the ousted Duke of Milan in *The Tempest*), and he is entitled to use any means available to him to restore the status quo, including that of using 'craft against vice' (III.2.265), disguise and eavesdropping. This is paralleled by the ***deus ex machina*** device used in classical literature, whereby the gods could appear among men to intervene and untie the knots and solve the impasses they get themselves into.

Hamlet is only an agent of divine providence, and there are things he may not know and understand, but the Duke could be said to be divine providence itself, given that he is omniscient, omnipotent and omnipresent. Like Prospero, he sets the play's action in motion, directs its course, and rescues it from tragedy. The question, as always in cases involving free will versus supernatural foreknowledge, is whether he actually causes the fall of Angelo by knowing that it will happen (which would then make him less sympathetic, like Milton's God), or whether he is simply his scourge and minister.

A variation on this interpretation is to claim that the Duke represents an ironical treatment of divine providence (see Palmer, p. 66). Like Iago in *Othello*, the Duke is a playwright who devises and allocates roles; but unlike Iago, the Duke finds his human material intractable and unamenable to following the script: Juliet, Angelo, Lucio and Barnardine are not susceptible to prediction and regulation (unlike Brabantio, Desdemona, Cassio, Roderigo and Othello).

Dark deeds darkly answered

There is an ambivalence about the Duke, which enables him to be seen as either hero or villain, icon of order or abrogator of responsibility. The 'meddling friar' (V.1.127) has aroused strong antipathy in many readers and audiences since the beginning of the twentieth century. Teachers, critics and students often find him morally repugnant, and he arouses as much debate as Isabella over his treatment of his fellow human beings.

The Penguin editor is particularly hard on the Duke, referring to his 'impotence and his irresponsibility' (introduction, p. 22) and claiming that politically 'the Duke is no less reprehensible than Angelo' (*ibid.*, p. 21). His critics dislike the way he takes it upon himself to play God, testing everyone and putting them on trial, and they find it impossible to forgive his apparent sadism in leaving Isabella in ignorance of her brother's rescue, his callous treatment of Juliet, and his telling Claudio to prepare himself for death when he knows he will not be executed. He also plays cat-and-mouse with Angelo, though with more justification, and all in all appears to have a 'supreme indifference to human feelings' (Muir, p. 113), like a scientist performing a controlled experiment on human nature.

As a father figure in both the priestly and regal roles, there is something distasteful in his proposal to his 'daughter' Isabella and his involvement in the sex life of his other 'daughter', Mariana. He either betrays confessional confidences or tells lies in claiming to be both Angelo's and Mariana's confessor. He has learnt of Isabella's predicament by eavesdropping, and there is an irony in his being a masked 'seemer' himself, in pretending to be a priest, intent on revealing hypocrisy in others. He is charged with capriciousness by Quiller-Couch (*The New Shakespeare* introduction, p. xxxiv) and of being consistent only in being inconsistent.

Testing virtue

However, if one disapproves of the Duke, one has to decide whether or not this is deliberate on Shakespeare's part, i.e. whether he is meant to be a dubious shadowy figure who gives rise to doubts about ethics and the nature of justice, or whether it is that tastes in rulers have changed since Shakespeare's day. His lack of warmth may be a failing, or it may be necessary for his elevated position (a dilemma of kingship Shakespeare deals with in many plays, including *Henry IV* and *King Lear*). Just as for Prospero, perhaps forgiveness is the most important, and most Christian, form of magnanimity.

In his role of restorer of order and values, the Duke must put virtue, honour and grace back in their places in traditional moral foundations. By telling Claudio that Isabella's honour caused her rightly to deny Angelo's attempt on her virtue, Claudio is given the opportunity to accept this and is thereby able to put himself back into a state of grace. Had he been told that he no longer faced death, he would not have been able to pass the test of his own metal; it is easy to give the right answer when nothing is at stake, just as it is easy to claim what decision one would make in circumstances one is unlikely ever to have to face, as Angelo does. As Milton put it, 'one cannot praise a fugitive and cloister'd virtue' (*Areopagitica*). Only when Claudio says that he will ask Isabella's pardon and welcome death does he deserve to be rewarded with his life. Likewise it is for the sake of her own salvation, earned through her ability to show mercy *in extremis*, that Isabella must be kept ignorant of her brother's reprieve.

In the Duke's further defence it may be said that, as Providence, he is committed to allowing time to take its course, necessary not only for dramatic **climax**, but for the change of characters' moral positions. He has the rare gift of self-knowledge (one much revered by Shakespeare, who shows a multitude of people in high places brought down by the lack of it) and not only accepts that he has been a lax ruler, but does something about it. By the end of the play the other characters, except Lucio, are able to view him as the traditional wise magistrate and benevolent monarch figure. A middle position on the Duke would be that he starts fallen and rises through endeavour and learning to his true position. The Penguin editor (commentary, p. 171) says that the change in the play at Act III scene 2 occurs because the Duke takes on an active role for the first time, as he at last begins 'to grasp the principles of good government'. As a man who has run out of ideas and become politically impotent, and one who acknowledges his defeat and spiritual bankruptcy, he is forced to embark on a process of self-education, learning from Isabella the difference between mercy and leniency in order to re-earn his title.

Angelo: angel with horns

Angelo says 'Let's write "good Angel" on the devil's horn' (II.4.16), referring to the paradoxical concept of a 'false seeming' devil who appears to be virtuous, like himself. He is, of course, also punning on his name, and possibly on the association of horns with rams, stags, cuckoldry and the devil's sexual prowess generally.

Pater asked of Angelo 'whether he is indeed psychologically possible' (Palmer, p. 57). In the source story Angelo is the embodiment of pure evil, and this may actually be the more questionable in terms of plausibility. Shakespeare does not deal in absolutes for moral and artistic reasons, and therefore his Angelo falls suddenly into corruption through a momentary contact with goodness, just as Leontes (*The Winter's Tale*) and Othello are shown to fall as suddenly into jealousy in their respective plays. Angelo is certainly psychologically possible according to the internal evidence of the play and as far as general literary convention is concerned. We are prepared for his fall by Claudio's assertion that Isabella has that kind of power over men, and by Lucio's viewing her as a 'saint'. She combines the powers of both words and vision, also warned against by the nun Francisca (I.4.12–13), so the audience should not be so surprised by Angelo's reaction to Isabella. There are biblical and folkloric literary traditions of young maids being able to breach the defences and wring the hearts of the proudest of men of the most hardened resolve, and of virgins inspiring lust and presenting an irresistible challenge. If one also takes into account that Angelo has previously dallied with Mariana and apparently intended to be married, and is therefore no celibate or renouncer of women, then it is even less surprising that he should be attracted to an impassioned Isabella.

Question of sympathy

The bigger question is whether the audience can feel sympathy for Angelo. He is given the role of the Player King, a doomed figure of shreds and patches, a shadow figure without substance who, like *Hamlet*'s Claudius, can never take the place of the real king, however hard he tries. Isabella is his nemesis, and if one has no sympathy for Isabella, or for the Duke, then one must feel that Angelo is their victim. He did not ask for promotion and was not free to refuse it; in fact, he asked that he should be tested further before given such a great responsibility. The Duke gave him a job he had failed to do himself, perhaps a job no mere human could do satisfactorily. Angelo is set up and used by the Duke to make himself more popular on his return. Desire corrupts even the strongest of men, and temptation has caused the fall of greater men than Angelo since the creation. It needs to be borne in mind that he commits no actual crime in the play, only in thought. A tortured human is not necessarily a villain, and the latter do not tend to agonise over their dilemma. All the play's **soliloquies** are his (one of Shakespeare's devices for evoking audience sympathy), in which he shares his anguish and gives an honest account of himself.

On the other hand, Angelo is one of Shakespeare's **Machiavels**: he practises ruthless self-interest and unethical methods to retain political power, which he relishes. His jilting of Mariana for personal gain predates his promotion to ruler of the city and therefore the core of weakness and evil is already within him and not caused by either the Duke or Isabella. Shakespeare does not allow him any attractive characteristics, unlike most of his other villains, and therefore sympathy for him is difficult to evoke. Chambers (quoted in Muir, p. 100) calls him 'a cold-hearted, self-righteous prig' even after his exposure. Angelo's dilemma is not one with which an audience, especially a modern one, can easily identify. He does not come well out of comparison with other characters; he is shown to be a lesser man than Claudio, who had no intention of abandoning his betrothed and 'known' wife for any reason, and even than Lucio, who makes no pretensions of being more than a fallible human with appetites. Angelo makes his own decisions and therefore the outcome is his own responsibility.

Precise Lord Angelo

Angelo dominates a play in which he rarely appears. His name is on virtually every page of the text, once ten times, and the other characters are obsessed with him because of what he represents to them, which is either the opposite of what they themselves believe in or is what they fear about the human condition. Here are some of the possibilities:

- fallible man, potentially divine but essentially fallen
- 'a fugitive and cloister'd virtue' (Milton) which is strong in theory but which fails in practice
- a willing spirit betrayed by weak flesh
- duty in conflict with desire, the fundamental dilemma situation
- the embodiment of Pride, the first and worst of the **seven deadly sins** and Satan's own

- the exemplification of a current idea on the Jacobean stage that every man is dominated by a particular humour whose excess destroys him; he is 'precise' (I.3.50) to a fault
- living proof that 'power tends to corrupt and absolute power corrupts absolutely' (Lord Acton)
- the overreacher, someone who is overconfident of his abilities, is guilty of **hubris**, and aims too high, inevitably to fall
- a 'seemer' and like all such in Shakespeare, he must be exposed and humiliated
- someone who should set an example for others to aspire to, but who fails; Claudio accepts his punishment until he learns that the judge is corrupt and above the law
- man as an island; he is unable to see outside himself and cannot imagine the feelings of others
- a male mirror image of Isabella the nun, who is therefore narcissistically attracted to himself in her
- the paradoxical danger of admiring virtue, whereby unattainable beauty and purity can evoke a desire which lures one towards his/her doom
- a repressed man cut off from humanity because of the experiences which he has denied himself
- a symbol of Vienna's illegal, lecherous and hypocritical ways
- a victim of male susceptibility to female beauty
- an example of the corrupting power of avarice, since he abandoned his betrothed for financial reasons

Dubious repentance

Whatever his role and crime, there remain the questions of whether Angelo's punishment is appropriate, and what one is to make of his reactions in the final judgement scene. If he has developed an antipathy to Mariana then having to marry her is indeed a punishment (on a par with Lucio having to marry Kate Keepdown), especially if he is wedded to the idea of womanly perfection as embodied by Isabella. From a legalistic and moral point of view, it is appropriate that he should make an honest woman of Mariana, and that women generally should be compensated for being the victims of men in the play.

His real punishment, however, lies in his fall from grace, from office, from the Duke's high regard, from his own self-esteem, and the consequent painful and public revaluation of himself, which he will have to live with. At the end he is still insisting on the subjugation of the personal to the law, which may be proof of his commitment to this principle. On the other hand, his reaction to being ignominiously exposed may be something which his personal pride cannot accept, since to accept forgiveness requires humility. Like Satan, and Shakespeare's Roman heroes, Angelo would literally rather die than kneel before a higher authority, though he acknowledges the Duke's 'power divine' (V.1.366). A stubborn pride makes Angelo prefer death to mercy, just as Antonio and Sebastian in *The Tempest* cannot bear to be forgiven by Prospero, and Iago and Shylock refuse to accept the authority of a Venice whose laws and prejudicial practices they despise. Angelo remains an unreasonable and isolated figure to the very end, like Malvolio in *Twelfth Night* and perhaps for the same reason: he feels aggrieved and still believes himself to be superior to everyone else.

The diabolical Lucio

Lucio's name, while being typical of Shakespeare's usage of Italian names, actually means 'light' and calls to mind Lucifer, the brightest and best of the angels who fell, because of a refusal to be subordinate, and became Satan. Lucio also shares with Satan a seductive tongue and strong appetites; almost every word he speaks in the play is a lie, and he is the link between eating, sexual temptation and fallen man. He also has a taste for war (I.2.13–15) because as a soldier he finds it profitable.

He is undoubtedly a destroyer of reputations, at least where Angelo and the Duke are concerned, and calumny was taken seriously in Jacobean times, not least by James I himself. Iago, arguably the most evil of Shakespeare's creations, destroys everyone else's reputation in *Othello*, and Lucio has touches of Iago in his attitudes to so-called goodness and to personal gain. Satan slandered God to the other angels and to Eve in order to foment division and rebellion in his own self-interest. Lucio is also guilty of lechery, one of the **seven deadly sins** (and arguably of several more), and has no respect for women, except possibly for the saintly Isabella because she isn't one in his eyes. His lifestyle is one of **Rabelaisian** ribaldry and bawdy, and his humour revolves around bodily functions and diseases. Furthermore, his notions of the duties of friendship are questionable, judging by his indifference to the plight of the arrested Pompey. He admits to being incapable of seriousness and that it is his 'familiar sin/With maids to seem the lapwing and to jest/Tongue far from heart' (I.4.31–33). Dissociation of word and feeling is considered a serious fault in other plays, such as *Hamlet*.

Ironic go-between

Like Iago, Lucio has a foot in all camps and can fraternise with all persons and ranks, which gives him an important plot function. He is not only an observer and social commentator on both the lowlife of the taverns and the behaviour of the higher orders, but he interferes in the action; he advises Isabella to return and beg of Angelo and is therefore the cause of the ensuing events. He has a verbal dexterity which is entertaining but alarming, since he reveals in his slanderous attacks on the Duke how words can be used as weapons and destroyers of truth. His revelling in sensual indulgence makes him the opposite of the precise and puritanical Angelo, and allows the irony that they commit a similar crime against a woman and receive the same punishment of having to restore her reputation. As an inveterate liar and scandalmonger he is meant to be the **antithesis** of the Duke, but his exaggerations and distortions shape themselves into a paradoxical kind of truth which must be faced — such as his describing Angelo as 'a man whose blood/Is very snow-broth' (I.4.57–58) — so that the audience has cause to reflect on the human types represented by the other characters and the extent to which they are guilty as charged.

He is a shifty character, as represented by his moving between verse and prose throughout the play. He represents amorality and what happens when there is no firm government; he evokes and tests a wide range of responses to the 'demigod Authority'; he is a lord of misrule, appropriate for a yuletide play, who enjoys reversing status and turning things upside down. The Penguin editor calls him 'the complete opportunist' (commentary, p. 180), who is a warning to the audience that such people are always with us, hovering on the edges of history looking for a chance of profit and entertainment. As he puts it: 'I am a kind of burr, I shall stick' (IV.3.175). Paradoxically, he uses the religious terms of 'grace' and 'sainted', apparently without irony, as if errant Lucios are validated by the existence of virtuous Isabellas, or that she has the power to subdue his tongue and inspire his reverence.

Charming villain

It cannot be denied that, as with so many of Shakespeare's villains, we find Lucio attractive. His showmanship, cheekiness and directness endear him to the audience; we enjoy his playing with words and we are glad he is spared the death penalty. He is the licensed fool of Shakespeare's other plays, comic and tragic, who can see through the pretensions of the high and mighty to their frail humanity and can offer an irreverent but recognisable perspective on them, as in his description of 'a meddling friar' (V.1.127) and 'the old fantastical Duke of dark corners' (IV.3.155–56). He is a warm character in a cold play, and one of the few we can identify with. He is a cynical survivor, like Feste in *Twelfth Night*, and is apparently unscathed and unchanged by his experiences in the play, which audiences find reassuring.

However, it is Lucio's relationship with the Duke which is the crucial issue. Barnardine and Lucio are the products of the Duke's years of misrule, which is perhaps why he has no authority over either of them. The Duke and Lucio might exchange places, for we are tempted to ask which is the judge and which is the thief, further adding to the ironies and complexities of the theme of justice. As the Duke's amusing adversary, Lucio steals sympathy from the Duke. He is the anti-Duke, his alter ego; they are linked by the plot and dialogue throughout the play, and Lucio has the last word before the Duke's closing speech. The low Lucio teaches the Duke his human frailties, as Caliban might have taught Prospero his in *The Tempest*. There are things of darkness to be acknowledged, chaotic elements which cannot be controlled by any power on earth and which will always lurk beyond the light. The

Duke and Lucio offer conflicting alternative visions of humanity and enact the clash of its opposing **Apollonian** and **Dionysiac** tendencies. The Duke would like to be the director of the play, but Lucio is the maverick actor who ad libs his lines and cannot be trusted to deliver the script as written. The antagonism between the two men is a rare source of comedy in the play, but also symbolises the serious opposition of light and dark, truth and falsehood and the superior seductive powers of the latter.

Isabella's dilemmas

Isabella is a novice nun of the order of St Clare, a monastic foundation whose dedication to chastity is betokened by their white habit. She has three moral dilemmas to deal with during the play: whether or not to submit to an indecent proposal; to aid and abet a sex act between a couple not actually married; to plead for the life of the supposed murderer of her brother. Isabella is a contradiction in terms, being confident, eloquent and passionate as well as naive, reclusive and passive, and she has a surprising number and range of relationships with the other characters. She is a novice nun to Francisca, a saint to Lucio, a sister and judge to Claudio, a temptress and saviour to Angelo, a pious maiden and future wife to the Duke, an exploiter and supporter of Mariana, a quasi sister-in-law to Juliet and aunt to her baby. These are incompatible roles in many cases, both within and between relationships, and all of them are ethically problematic, making her the focal point of interest of the play, for Angelo, the Duke and Claudio, as well as for the audience. She is also the main point of spiritual interest in that as a virgin and nun her chastity is the basis of her relationship with the church, and it is her chosen role as a designated bride of Christ which underlies her speech and behaviour, and therefore the plot of the play.

Hostile reactions

There is no other Shakespeare character whom critics, including females, have found so unsympathetic or condemned so violently. Isabella has been accused of being too pious and not pious enough, being icy cold and too fierce and fiery. The consensus is that though she is the heroine, she is disappointing. It is not only a modern disgust which has been expressed; as early as 1753 Charlotte Lennox (see *The New Shakespeare* introduction, p. xxviii) attacked Isabella for 'the manners of an affected prude, outrageous in her seeming virtue; not of a pious, innocent and tender mind'. Hazlitt (*ibid.*, p. xxix) was 'not greatly enamoured of Isabella's rigid chastity, though she could not have acted otherwise than she did'. Sir George Greenwood (*ibid.*, p. xxix) also agrees with her decision, but laments that she did not deliver it in a more 'restrained and measured language, more in sorrow than in anger, and not with the abuse and vituperation of a termagant'. Quiller-Couch declares: 'To put it nakedly, she is all for saving her own soul, and she saves it by turning … into a bare procuress' (*ibid.*, p. xxx). But as Stella Gonet (actor of Isabella in the 1994 RSC production) explains: 'The problem of doing this play nowadays is that people just can't understand the importance that Isabella attaches to being sexually pure… Isabella would lay down her life for her brother but she can't give up her body.'

Case for the prosecution

Isabella's way of thinking is associated with Angelo's cold and legalistic approach to life and relationships, and her wanting 'more strict restraint' (I.4.4) is evidence of the sin of pride in that she desires to prove that she can go beyond the endurance of normal mortals. Her denial of the pleasures and pains of the flesh makes her seem excessively austere, and she evinces the typical zeal and elation of the Christian martyr who is eager to offer self and others for sacrifice in the cause of an ideal. Her brand of Christianity, however, seems to lack the leavening of charity and to have more in common with Old Testament retribution. She is quick to recommend death, believing Mariana as well as Claudio would be better off dead. It is perhaps hypocritical of her to refuse sex for herself but find it acceptable to use Mariana for that purpose, and to save one's own honour at the expense of another's is of dubious morality.

Because Claudio has the affection of his friends and the love of his betrothed, Isabella's treatment of him seems too severe by comparison; she goes against the traditional bond of brother and sister in literature, which is usually a strong and cherishing one. The lukewarm way in which she pleads for Claudio to Angelo initially and so easily gives up suggests that she doesn't really care about Claudio, as does her quick dismissal of his reasonable desire to live. What could be her last words to him, when she turns her back on him still pleading, are harsh: ''Tis best thou diest quickly' (III.1.154). So too is the line: 'Then, Isabel, live chaste, and, brother, die' (II.4.184). Like Lady Macbeth, she applies emotional blackmail when she accuses Claudio of being cowardly and dishonourable, less than a man, and threatens to withdraw her love and respect for him. She does not seem to experience grief over his supposed death (which compares unfavourably with the response of other Shakespeare heroines, such as Viola, to similar situations), she pleads for Angelo's life though she believes he is her brother's murderer, and she does not apparently show any joy at the discovery that her brother is still alive.

Case for the defence

Only through the extreme of adversity can one be tested, and it is Isabella's providential role to test her brother, her sisterly role to be her brother's keeper. Isabella saves Claudio's soul in Christian terms by making him resolute for death: 'Whosoever will save his life shall lose it' (Matthew 10:34). She sincerely believes that 'Better it were a brother died at once/Than that a sister, by redeeming him, /Should die for ever' (II.4.106–07) — better for him as well as for her. That she would sooner die than lose her virginity and that she would gladly die to save her brother are not just rhetorical claims. To comply with Angelo's proposal would be to commit a deadly sin, the punishment for which was believed then and now by the Roman Catholic church to be eternal damnation and burning in hell; she genuinely believes that her immortal soul is at stake. She fears that if she enters the debate and listens to the tempter, in the form of either Angelo or Claudio, she will be lost as Eve was to the words of Satan. Chambers (Muir, p. 94) makes it clear that Christian duty through the ages has meant being willing to sacrifice blood ties for the sake of righteousness. Isabella feels that 'The honour of her family and her religion are more to her than mere life, her own or Claudio's' (*ibid.*, p. 95). As well as biblical models, such as Abraham and Isaac, there are classical precedents for valuing a higher good over a family relationship.

Like a lonely fairytale orphan she has no parents to guide her, her brother has obviously been engaged elsewhere, and the nunnery may be the only home on offer. A further ironic complexity is that it was the duty of a brother, especially in the absence of a father, to protect the virginity of his sister. She is simply trying to obey and apply the vows of chastity of her adopted order; it, not she, is responsible if they are inhumane. It is not her idea to visit Angelo; she is a political pawn in a man's world, and that Angelo views her as just a body to be bought proves the difficulties to be faced as a woman and the reasons for wishing to become a nun. At the time a virgin, let alone a would-be nun, would have been terrified of sexual intercourse, and of the possibility of becoming pregnant, and she rightly suspects that in any case her sacrifice could be in vain as Angelo might not keep his word and no one would believe her word against his. It is not her fault that she is caught up in sexual liaisons between her brother and his 'beloved', between Angelo and his 'betrothed', and is forced to make decisions in each case which affect the outcome of their relationship.

She can separate the sin from the sinner, which is a definition of compassion, and she does in fact express anger and weep in Act IV scene 3 when the Duke tells her that Claudio is dead. Her asking for mercy for Angelo could be interpreted as an admission that she was too hard on her brother and has learnt from her mistake. In any case, Angelo is technically innocent of the crime for which he has been sentenced to death, whereas Claudio freely admitted his guilt and Juliet was visible evidence of it. It is difficult to imagine another response that Isabella could have given to Angelo's demand which would have been any more palatable to the audience or would have earned its respect.

Complexity

It is not a simple case of comparing modern liberal to contemporary Christian attitudes. Shakespeare's audience would have been as much exercised as we are as to whether we can approve of Isabella putting her chastity above her brother's life, even though the importance of female purity was obviously much greater then than now, at least as an ideal. Shakespeare should arguably be given credit for deliberately creating a controversial heroine and manipulating the audience's response to her (as he does with Ophelia in *Hamlet* and Desdemona in *Othello*) by making her alternately pitiable and cruel when under pressure, and therefore more psychologically convincing. Ironically, the valuation of women according to their chastity, honour and reputation is a man-made measuring device. Men make the laws and enforce them, and are the arbiters of acceptable social behaviour in females. There are still countries in the world where men stone women to death for the supposed sexual promiscuity which Isabella rejects.

Whetstone's heroine in *Promos and Cassandra* (see Palmer, p. 106) chooses to give herself as an act of self-sacrifice inviting deepest admiration, so that though the heroine may be divided the audience is free from doubt. Shakespeare chose to do it the other, and more interesting, way round, demanding the audience's engagement and reflection on the moral dilemma and suggesting that there is no right answer. It is the very fact that Isabella does not see her choice as problematic which suggests that Shakespeare wants us to find it so. The audience is likely to go through 'a sequence of opposed feelings' (Palmer, p. 97) towards Isabella, of attraction and repulsion, which alternately engages and alienates our sympathy for her. Real humans often have this effect on others, and those who find her difficult are perhaps missing the point. Her complexity (compared to the simple Mariana) is partly the cause of the perplexity she has caused audiences and critics; her ability to grasp issues and think quickly and adapt to people and situations, despite her youth and lack of experience of men and public life, is perhaps evidence of a depth rather than a shallowness of perception and emotion.

Isabella's development

Rossiter claims that 'Shakespeare's fault lies in giving Isabella no transitions' (p. 162), so that the Isabella who solves her second dilemma by readily conniving with the Duke over an apparently similar transgression can be seen as inconsistent with the earlier one who condemned her brother's offence. This can be explained, however, by it being the Friar/Duke's suggestion and therefore sanctioned by the church, and by the existence of a previous contract which would have appealed to her respect for the law. Perhaps the audience is meant to appreciate that she has matured from the extreme adolescent who wanted 'a more strict restraint' (I.4.4) than a nunnery could offer to someone able to respond less dogmatically, having had her ideas modified by painful experience in the interim. She may even have realised that 'Chastity without Charity shall be chained in hell' (Milton, *Areopagitica*). Wilson Knight (quoted in Palmer, p. 109) claimed that she changes during the course of the play 'from sanctity to humanity' and learns to deal with real people rather than with abstract principles.

Isabella's third dilemma, which takes her more time to decide about than the other two, is whether to plead for mercy for Angelo. After the third summons she does so, proving herself to possess Christian magnanimity and forgiveness, since she believes her brother to be dead because of Angelo, and (unlike in all the sources) she is not pleading for her own new husband's life but for someone else's, which makes it a true act of charity devoid of self-interest. Isabella has been re-educated in the 'function of virtue as an active force in the world' (*Arden* introduction, p. lxxxii) rather than as a passive resistance, and her tongue is kindled to passionate eloquence rather than legalistic sermonising for the first time.

Isabella's final silence

Isabella's silence for over 80 lines at the end of the play, and her failure to respond to the Duke's repeated offer of marriage and possible fourth dilemma — abbess or duchess? — poses a difficulty for the audience, as well as for the play's director and the actor playing Isabella: what are her movements, body language and facial expressions during all this time? Critics are outraged both by her being frozen in a state of shock and by her undergoing a transformation from a stern nun to a conventional heroine who casts off her habit and falls into the arms of the Duke, since the former interpretation is against the spirit of comedy and the latter is unprincipled and inconsistent with all her previous moral posturing. One must assume, however, that she does finally decline 'coyly into the ex-Friar's bosom' (Rossiter, p. 162), as the conventions of comedy require an ending which involves a triple marriage. It could be argued that neither she nor the Duke are fitting or convincing aspirants to that state, given their previous convictions and the failure of the plot to prepare us for this moment, but a union of mercy and truth, as symbolised by Isabella and the Duke, is fitting for a play performed at Christmas, when the birth of a child is meant to embody both spiritual concepts, and celibacy and chastity have no role to play at this time of year. One could argue that the woman is revealed beneath the nun's attire as surely as all other disguises are thrown off in the dénouement, or that there is nothing for Isabella to say, since she cannot refuse the wishes of her 'prince'.

Possible feminist ways of playing the ending are: that Isabella does not actually hear the Duke, because she is distracted by Claudio's presence and has gone to his side; that she shows only by her expression the anger she feels at the Duke's presumption and her continuing subjection to the desires of men and need for suppression of her own; that she pulls her veil over her face to show her acknowledgement that becoming a wife is equal to becoming a nun (in both states women lose their freedom of speech and are required to listen and obey with a 'willing ear', V.1.533). That Mariana is also wearing a veil, which she can only remove at her lord's command, is further support for this interpretation, the metaphor visually reinforced by the physical opening and closing of the garment used to conceal the faces of brides and nuns and repressed women through the ages. Speech is a method of female rebellion in Shakespeare (see Emilia's end in *Othello*) and if Isabella is now subjugating herself, whether from choice or necessity, silence would be the most appropriate gesture.

Women in the play

Virgins, wives, widows and whores

The female characters in the play — Isabella, Mariana, Juliet and Mistress Overdone, plus the invisible Kate Keepdown — convey singly and collectively a strong impression of the lives of women at the time of the setting and the writing of the play. The women are united and divided (as are the three women in *Othello*) by their theory and practice in the disposition of their bodies. The possible roles for women of the time were to be virgins/nuns, wives/mothers, widows, or whores, all options defined by their sexual and therefore financial relationship with men, which in turn determines their social status (whereas men were defined first and foremost by their jobs, and secondly by their political and religious affiliations). In the play all of these women are or become dependent on men for their well-being, and even survival, which in turn determines the way in which they are perceived by men, and therefore by society as a whole.

Female dependency

Prostitution was the result of financial need and of women having nothing else to sell but their own bodies. Children of a casual relationship can be denied or ignored by the father, as Lucio demonstrates, but not by the mother, who bears the physical and social stigma of pregnancy, and must feed the child or watch it starve. Juliet claims that she is equally responsible for the creation of a child, but is not credited with equality and is treated more leniently than Claudio since she is considered his moral and intellectual inferior, as Eve was to Adam. Mariana is ruined for life if she cannot get Angelo to make an honest woman of her, though it was no fault of hers but a failed business transaction between her brother and her would-be husband which caused her exclusion from society.

Isabella may have religious conviction, but she is also attempting to opt out of a patriarchal society by taking the veil, or to win some respect through her penitential piety. Either way, she is an indictment of the system which can offer a young, healthy and intelligent female only a forced marriage (always an arrangement between father or brother and suitor) or life (non-life) in a nunnery. Her decision is in any case rescinded in the final scene by the countermand of the Duke, who claims her for his own without reference to, or response from, her. Angelo tells Isabella to put on the 'destined livery' of women, with its implication of servitude. The inevitable conclusion is that women not only do not have the power to legislate or even speak (and are dependent upon the, often whimsical, dictates of the males who do) but that they have no say in or control over the course of their own lives. The same impression is conveyed in the exact contemporary play, *Othello*.

Though many other Shakespeare plays carefully ignore the personal and social products of sex, i.e. pregnancy, children and prostitution, *Measure for Measure* makes them a central and thematic issue. The women are paired in various combinations to draw attention to sexual status, marital contracts and seduction strategies, and the audience will note similar consequences across the social classes and professions from nun to whore. For example, both Mariana and Kate Keepdown rely on an enforced marriage to make them socially acceptable and financially secure. The play could be said to be predominantly about women in that it highlights both their lack of power and the way in which they are blamed for bringing men down and the city into disrepute through sexual allure (though note it is the parasitical Pompeys and opportunistic Lucios who are enjoying the benefits). Insofar as Isabella is the heroine and main focus of plot interest — and arguably the most complex character — and since, as a comedy, the play must deal with marriage, the play is about women and how they are affected by the causes and effects of seduction, prostitution and broken nuptial agreements. However, though it touches on the impact of the private on the public, it is the political arena which is overtly being explored in the play, and this is firmly controlled by men and their official positions and job titles.

Saving graces

As in other Shakespeare comedies, the men are redeemed by the women in the play, both as humans and as Christians. Claudio, Angelo and Lucio are dragged down into psychic degradation through physical lack of control; Mariana and Isabella, through the offices of the Duke who recognises and harnesses their stereotypically female qualities, raise each other and the rest of the cast to spiritual rehabilitation. Men represent both crime and justice, paradoxically, leaving vacant for women the position of charity, which brings redemption to both the giver and the receiver. Mercy and forgiveness are recommended and dispensed by the female characters in many Shakespeare plays, for example Portia in *The Merchant of Venice* and Cordelia in *King Lear*. The tender virtues which any society needs in order to thrive are invested in its women; even Mistress Overdone has kept Lucio's child at her own expense out of the goodness of her heart.

St Paul opined that it was better to marry than to burn (in hell for the sin of lechery), and therefore, biblically speaking, women redeem the souls of men by making possible both marriage and the bringing forth of children and hope into the world. Individually they redeem men by softening and transforming them through their unconditional and unjudging love; the Duke has had his 'complete bosom' (I.3.3) pierced by Isabella, and we are meant to believe that Mariana, who believes 'best men are moulded out of faults' (V.1.436), and wants no better man, will do the same for Angelo. Isabella's progress through the play could be seen, like that of Katherina in *The Taming of the Shrew*, as a shift from a male stance (aggressive, argumentative, objective) to a female one (sympathetic, subservient, subjective), so that she redeems herself as a woman as well as revealing demi-gods to be no more than men.

Justice, law and order

Justice versus mercy, human passions versus the restraint of law, were regular topics of discussion and concern among educated Elizabethans and Jacobeans, and were thought to directly relate to the practical matter of good government, as well as abstractly to religious beliefs. This issue is announced in the Duke's first line: 'Of government the properties to unfold…'. Isabella begs for justice four times in Act V scene 1 line 25.

Judgement and judges

The primary meaning of the title and main theme of the play is to do with justice, how one measures and dispenses it, and its relationship to judgement and therefore to the qualities of the judge. Theological, social, and political structures were based on the concept of a hierarchy headed by a ruler or primary being who had the right to play God over fellow men, and who was therefore expected to be better than them, though only a human. Many of Shakespeare's plays, both comedies and tragedies, specifically address the inherent paradoxes and complexities of this theme, such as *The Merchant of Venice* and *King Lear*.

Contemporary essayists and statesmen were much exercised by the dilemma of how to match the punishment to the crime, and how to preserve the law's majesty, undermined in the play by Abhorson, Elbow, and Pompey, the lowlife administrators of justice. The Duke, Angelo, Escalus and the Provost are the judges, but they are also fallible and therefore call into question the law's integrity, man's right to judge fellow men, and the difference, if any, between the judge and the criminal. Though justice is apparently re-established at the end of the play, this is only a dramatic illusion and convention, and not necessarily fully convincing for the audience, or even all of those on stage. In several other plays, such as *Twelfth Night*, *The Merchant of Venice* and *The Tempest*, there are characters still disaffected and unreconciled as the curtain falls.

Law and order

Shakespeare's contemporaries were terrified of a return to civil war, still mindful of the bloody Wars of the Roses between the houses of Lancaster and York, which came to an end only in 1487. They therefore set a high value on civil order and decorum on the streets, which is threatened in Vienna by the behaviour of the bawds and tapsters. Laws were seen as the means of imposing orderly behaviour on the masses, and their enforcement was a bulwark not only against crime but against anarchy, rebellion and unbridled self-indulgence. Behaviour likely to cause a breach of the peace, disorderly conduct, and many of the other laws still on the English statute books are a legacy of the perceived need to curb and refuse to give licence to public unruliness in any shape or form.

The Devil was seen in disorder, hence the importance of order. The head should rule the heart, reason should control appetite: these were the fundamental tenets of the medieval church and sixteenth- and seventeenth-century society (and the Fall of Man was quoted as the original example of how sin enters where the reverse is allowed to occur). It follows from this that goodness is passive and evil is active, that law and order are therefore a retreating from rather than an embracing of what life has to offer by way of sensual pleasure. Isabella wants more restraint, and Lucio wants less.

Old and New Testaments

The two sections of the Bible offer very different views of justice. The emphasis of the Old Testament is on 'An eye for an eye and a tooth for a tooth' and 'Do unto others as they would do unto you' — i.e. reciprocal punishment and revenge — and on the necessity for suffering in order to be redeemed from the sin of Adam. The New Testament preaches the Christian precepts of mercy and forgiveness, based on an understanding of human ignorance — Christ's words on the cross being 'Father, forgive them; for they know not what they do' — and on the sacrifice of laying down one's life for another: 'Greater love hath no man than this, that a man lay down his life for his friends.' The Christian admonition to respond to insult or injury by turning the other cheek is the opposite of the Old Testament practice of righteous anger and making enemies pay for their crimes. In *Measure for Measure* the two systems clash, both between characters and within the character of Isabella.

The quality of mercy

Pontius Pilate allows the crowd to choose which criminal is to be shown clemency, Christ or Barabbas, and they make the wrong choice, but the principle is clear: mercy is a virtue. However, the alternative viewpoint, as espoused by Angelo and also uttered by Escalus, is that mercy makes a mockery of the judicial system. For these characters, it is better to overpunish someone and make an example which may save others from the same sin, than to show leniency and pardon a criminal, which may lead others into vice. These arguments still divide political parties and religions nowadays. There was a strong lobby in Shakespeare's society that mercy was a divine attribute (since God showed mercy to Adam and Eve when he commuted their death sentence and gave them the chance of re-earning eternal life), symbolised by the very existence of Christ, and that therefore rulers should follow the example

from on high. As Portia says in *The Merchant of Venice*: 'the quality of mercy is not strain'd,/It droppeth as the gentle rain from heaven.'

Capital crime and punishment

The death penalty was much employed in Shakespeare's time, often for offences that we would consider minor, such as suspected witchcraft or trivial theft. In the hierarchy of crimes, treason has always been considered the worst — as a betrayal of a whole nation — followed by murder. Beheading was the punishment for aristocratic and gentleman murderers, whereas hanging was for common felons. The false logic underpinning the laws of Vienna is that if murder, i.e. the taking away of a life, is a capital offence, then the illegitimate creation of a life should be regarded as equally heinous, given that both are powers invested only in the law and the church, upholders of state and faith as interpreters of God's will, and not in individual man and his passing inclinations.

The spirit or the letter?

Pater coined the concept of a 'finer justice' (Palmer, p. 61), one based on love and a recognition of 'the true conditions of men and things', which is different from and more palatable than a justice based on rights and facts. Laws can only describe abstract conditions, not the human elements which constitute them, and one of the debates which always rage around the topic of justice is whether it is better to 'cut a little/Than fall, and bruise to death' (II.1.5–6), and whether one should apply blanket prescriptions which make no distinction between persons, or whether each case should be considered on its merits and take into account mitigating or aggravating circumstances. The general tendency has always been towards the former (for which reason previous convictions cannot be mentioned during a trial in an English courtroom), but paradoxically character references can be admitted, and in practice the outcome is often influenced by extraneous influences such as gender, class, dress and physical appearance.

Angelo argues forcibly for the exact implementation of the law in *Measure for Measure*, whereas Isabella suggests that the crime not the person should be judged, and other characters take up positions in between these extremes. There is a suspicion expressed or implied in all of Shakespeare's plays that rough justice is a very blunt tool, capable of at best a lack of precision and at worst miscarriage, and that it therefore needs to be tempered with something more refined, based more on the spirit and less on the letter of the law. As Rossiter says (p. 153), 'in *Measure for Measure* nobody questions that justice itself is on trial'.

The play poses a huge number of philosophical questions and moral dilemmas, all arising from the concept and definition of justice, with many occurring in Act I. You may wish to consider some or all of these issues and whether they are still as controversial and topical today as they were then:

1 Can and should one human being judge another?
2 Does any judge have the right to impose the death penalty?
3 Do severe laws create a better society?
4 Can we judge a fellow human by appearances?
5 Should laws be applied or reactivated retrospectively?
6 Should a judge ever abdicate his authority?
7 Can the end justify the means?
8 Should absurd laws be obeyed?
9 Should the law be proactive or reactive in relation to human behaviour?
10 Should one expect higher standards of humans in positions of power?
11 Should social class be taken into account when sentencing?
12 Is the tempter to blame for the fall of the tempted?
13 Should allowances be made for previous good conduct?
14 Is ignorance of the law an acceptable defence?
15 Should principles be abandoned in a matter of life and death?
16 Should someone be harshly punished to deter others?
17 Does the state have a right to determine sexual conduct?
18 Does showing mercy bring justice into disrepute?
19 Can one distinguish between punishing the crime and the criminal?
20 Is a good motive a mitigating circumstance for a criminal action?
21 Is intention to commit a crime as culpable as actually committing it?
22 Is the conception of an illegitimate child in any sense a crime?
23 Should there be a legal category called 'crime of passion'?
24 Should crimes be viewed as relative or absolute?
25 Should a crime be pardoned if it was committed to avoid a more serious one?
26 Can slander or libel be equated with murder?
27 Should a person who denies the validity of the law be made subject to it?
28 Should secular law derive from religious beliefs?

Themes

As with other aspects of the play, binary oppositions are reflected within the themes, and one could say that opposition is in itself a main theme. Birth, marriage and death are fundamental aspects of humanity which can be treated humorously and mockingly or seriously and sentimentally, and both aspects are evident in *Measure for Measure*, which contains episodes of **black comedy**. Many of the themes are also built into the settings of the play, so that, for instance, metaphorical imprisonment is represented by the scenes which take place in prison, and physical abstinence is symbolised by a nunnery.

Opposites

The thematic contrasts upon which the play is built are:

- law vs anarchy
- celibacy vs lechery
- mercy vs justice
- heaven vs earth
- mind vs body
- mortality vs immortal soul
- laxity vs severity
- puritanism vs liberalism

- passion vs reason
- love vs lust
- individual vs state
- vice vs virtue
- penalty vs pardon
- liberty vs restraint
- divinity vs bestiality
- birth vs death

Matters of life and death

Conception and execution is the main polarity upon which the play turns — the giving and taking away of life — and many of the play's characters are involved in one or both processes. For instance, Juliet, Kate and Elbow's wife are or have been recently pregnant, Claudio and Lucio are impregnators, and Pompey a facilitator of conception. Claudio, Angelo, Lucio and Barnardine are sentenced to death but reprieved, Ragozine is not so lucky, and Abhorson and Pompey play executioner.

Other characters refer to procreation and death and use imagery for both themes throughout the play, for example Lucio describes Angelo as 'ungenitured' (III.2.164). Sometimes the two are combined, as when Claudio refers to death as an encounter with 'darkness as a bride/And hug it in mine arms' (III.1.87–88). Death and sexual embrace are commonly associated in literature, as evidenced by the use at this time of the verb 'to die' to mean to achieve orgasm, and the cutting off of heads is punningly suggestive of the loss of maidenheads. Exposure to the fear of death and exposure to the sexual act were both male rites of passage, and there is much use of the verb 'to make' in the play in both contexts. A man has to be both fit to live (and breed) and fit to die (be 'absolute for death', III.1.5), unlike Barnardine who fails on both counts.

Claudio, a gentlemen but also a man in the street, puts the social and legal system to the test by being involved in both the procreation and termination aspects of the law. The play's unplanned pregnancy is its focal point, commented upon by a nun, a pimp, a Puritan, a whoremonger, a magistrate and a Duke. The opinions given on this perennially common situation and aspect of human nature cover the range of possible negative religious, legal and social responses, and touch on all the themes and images of the play.

The themes question the nature, validity and limitations of humanity in isolation and within society, and the difficulties and anomalies of legislating for the regulation of sexual behaviour, which is where the personal and the political meet. The conflicting desires, needs and practices of men and women are explored, and of men and their office, for example judge, priest, provost, duke, executioner. The fraught relationships between the temporal and the spiritual, and between the higher and lower classes of society, are also highlighted. The rule of law is exposed as being fragile and dependent upon the premise that the nobility have the right to dictate and to punish only as long as they can prove themselves to be better than the common man.

Other themes

Temptation — can take the form of sex out of wedlock and brothels. Convents and prisons are refuges from/punishments for temptation. Isabella tempts Angelo and the Duke, in different ways. Failure to resist temptation by a woman caused the Fall of Man. Words and beauty are the two possible vehicles of temptation (II.2.177–79), so speaking and showing one's face simultaneously are prohibited by the St Clare order. Temptation leads to perdition, the loss of the immortal soul, a fear which much exercises Isabella and Angelo.

Substitution — such as a Mariana for an Isabella (bed trick), a Ragozine for a Claudio (head trick), or 'An Angelo for Claudio' (V.1.406). The Duke is God's representative and substitute on earth. The Duke makes Angelo his 'substitute' in Vienna. Lucio substitutes Friar Lodowick for himself when blaming him for slandering the Duke. Angelo fails to put himself in the place of Claudio when he condemns him.

Deception — such as 'seeming', hypocrisy and betrayal. Lucifer/Lucio betrayed God/the Duke. Disguise is a form of deliberate deception. In Shakespeare's plays the truth-seekers adopt self-absenting disguise, whereas the evil-doers are self-imposing deceivers.

Error — is different from evil, which is perpetrated knowingly. 'To err is human, to forgive divine' (Pope). Most of the characters make errors of judgement, for which they are judged and forgiven by the divine representative, the Duke. A character incapable of error, as Angelo at first appears to be, would not be human. Lucio, however, refuses to acknowledge the error of his ways.

Judgement — is a relevant concept to the play in all its senses: ability to rationalise and choose right from wrong; understand one's own and others' characters; being fit to condemn and punish oneself and others. Angelo is commanded to be 'judge/Of your own cause' (V.1.166–67). Everyone in the play, however lowly, passes judgement on everyone else from beginning to end, which gives us different judgements on the same character to complicate audience response.

Reputation — is the most valued asset of women and men in high places; slander is its enemy, and an example of the destructive power of words. Lucio's speciality is defamation of character. Angelo slanders Mariana and takes away her ability to live in society. Satan slandered God to Eve.

Oaths — have an important plot function and take the form in the play of nuptial contracts, nun's vows and verbal promises, such as Angelo gives to Isabella about Claudio. They are important as a motivation for quests and battles in biblical, mythological and romance literature. It destabilises society and relationships not to respect and keep oaths; their breaking is a betrayal. They have religious significance, as heaven is their witness, and are a way of testing integrity. The Duke keeps all his promises, for example that Isabella shall have her revenge and that Lucio will answer one day for his slanders. Lucio 'was fain to forswear' (IV.3.169) having got a wench with child, which distinguishes him from those who do keep their oaths or intend to, such as Claudio, who 'was ever precise in promise-keeping' (I.2.74–75). Barnardine takes an oath: 'I swear I will not die today for any man's persuasion' (IV.3.58), and this overrules the judicial decision that he will.

Moderation — the middle way (*via media*) was an Aristotelian ideal; the Duke is 'a gentleman of all temperance' (III.2.227), whereas other characters offend this golden mean by demanding 'more strict restraint' (I.4.4) and indulging in 'immoderate use' (I.2.126). In Shakespeare's plays, any form of extreme or excess (which includes both celibacy and lechery) leads to actual or potential disaster.

Testing — occurs in many forms. Claudio and Lucio test the system of justice, and the integrity of the three judges. Just as metal is tested for baseness or purity and judged by its weight in the scales, so are the characters each tested for their 'mettle', i.e. genuineness and therefore worth, in terms of their humanity and honesty. The ultimate form of test, on earth as it is in heaven, is a trial.

Silence — lies in opposition to the power of words. It can be seen as something to be valued, but also as a position of weakness. There are wronged and silent women in the play, who have no voice until given one by the Duke. The convent and the prison, both retreats from the world, enforce silence, and those on trial may only speak when addressed and then only to answer the specific question. Silence is a form of respect and submission, and the Duke finds it difficult to get Lucio to hold his tongue. Garrulousness, a form of lack of control, is associated in literature with lax morality and specifically sexual promiscuity. Though Isabella is granted a voice, with which she arouses Angelo and wins the Duke, she is reduced to silence at the end of the play.

Chastity — is opposed to charity in Isabella's first dilemma. Men desire virgins, but only as conquests; they accuse chaste maidens of frigidity (refusers of their 'destined livery', II.4.138) or inhumanity (things 'enskied and sainted', I.4.34), but abuse unchaste females and call them 'punks'. So women are damned if they do and damned if they don't in the eyes of the Lucios and Angelos, and the Christian church could also only come to terms with Mary the wife and mother if she were also a virgin. Isabella's white habit not only signifies that she is a nun, but that she is chaste (a virgin) and therefore pure. Since reproduction is natural, chastity is questioned in the play as an unnatural state, and Isabella is finally reclaimed for humanity, wifedom and motherhood, just as the Duke is reclaimed from his celibacy (renunciation of marriage).

Images

Shakespeare's imagery repays close study as each play has its own peculiar and recurring group of images in addition to the typical and traditional images of the Jacobean period, such as those pertaining to heaven and hell, fire and water, light and dark. Image and theme are closely related in Shakespeare plays, and one is often the concrete version of the other, for example Isabella's white habit is a metaphor for her purity of body and spirit, the prison bars denote the idea of restraint. In addition to reinforcing themes, imagery gives atmosphere and progression to a text, helps to delineate character, and provides integrity, pattern and meaning.

Black and white — as in Shakespeare's tragedies of the same decade, the colour scheme of black and white is dominant, with Isabella wearing a white habit and Angelo, as dignitary and Puritan, necessarily dressed in black, as are the friars. This suggests extremes of belief and behaviour between the characters and creates stark contrasts and paradoxes, for example Angelo and Lucio have names suggesting white or light but behaviour which may be seen as dark; life for Barnardine means a dark hole, but death for Claudio is a region of ice. The play's characters attempt to see things in clear and simple terms of black and white, but have to learn that humanity and society are more complex, that the borderlines are unclear, and that there are grey areas between control and tyranny, chastity and inhumanity, providence and chance, discipline and repression, mercy and laxity, belief and fanaticism, love and lust, execution and murder, law and justice.

Coins — are images stamped on metal which have value, and can be compared to human beings. The imagery of coins links the themes of procreation (minting), disguise (counterfeiting) and testing (the **pun** metal/mettle), and actualises the metaphor of weight and measure. Complete opposites can paradoxically be represented on two sides of the same coin, for example nuns and prostitutes, angels and devils. Money lent in usury will increase itself, connected to the idea of procreation as a form of spawning. Thus the usurer, to Jacobean minds, was a pimp who profits from the lechery of money, the basis of capitalism being that money breeds. Angelo's name, as well as having religious connotations, is that of an English coin, ironically the noble, which depicted an image of St Michael slaying the dragon, i.e. of good defeating evil. It was in use until the mid-seventeenth century and often punned upon.

Family terms — the Duke as friar is 'father', and is a father figure to Mariana and Isabella, both of whom he calls daughter (e.g. IV.3.110); Isabella as a nun is a sister, as well as being Claudio's sister, a notional sister to Mariana, and Juliet's sister-in-law; Provost refers to Barnardine hypothetically as a brother (IV.2.59), Escalus refers to 'my brother Angelo' (III.2.198) and his 'brother-justice' (III.2.241). The Duke calls Claudio 'my brother too' in the final scene (line 490), and insists on addressing Angelo as 'cousin'. 'Mother' is used for mother superior (I.4.86). Isabella reminds Claudio of what is owed to their father. These terms of blood and spiritual relationship give the play a biblical and religious quality which echoes the well-known precepts and injunctions of the Ten Commandments and loving thy brother as thyself, not being one's brother's keeper, laying down one's life for one's brother etc. They also convey the necessity for humanity to recognise and honour its social and moral bonds with others.

Weighing — is linked to scales, a symbol of justice, for example 'scaled' (III.1.255); 'my false o'erweighs your true' (II.4.170); 'then was your sin of heavier kind than his' (II.3.28); 'unweighing fellow' (III.2.132); 'sinister measure' (III.2.232); 'self-offences weighing' (III.2.254); 'you weigh equally' (IV.2.27); 'heavy middle of the night' (IV.1.34). False coins were believed to be lightweight, which connects with the imagery of counterfeiting and illegitimacy and ties in to the theme of measuring, testing and judging. Equal scales represent balance, one of the ideals of the play (personified by the appropriately named Escalus, who stands between the laxity of the Duke and the severity of Angelo).

Ice — it is said of Angelo, to denote his lack of humanity, that 'his urine is congealed ice' (III.2.104) and that he was 'a marble' to Mariana's tears (III.1.231). Hell is unusually described as a 'region of thick-ribbed ice' (III.1.126) by Claudio, and Lucio reprimands Isabella for being 'too cold' (II.2.45). Chastity is associated with the image cluster of icy words — white, pure and frigid — in opposition to the warm 'prompture of the blood' (II.4.178) which, in the heat of the moment, allows fiery passion and sexual ardour to thaw resistance and melt reason.

Imprisonment — is both literal and metaphorical: prison, convent and moated grange, as well as the constraint of religious principles, vows, contracts and laws. Licentiousness is the opposite, the freedom to roam, but restraint follows from too much liberty. Several of the scenes are set in prison and almost all of the characters appear there or are threatened with it. Marriage is a form of imprisonment (as denoted by the term wedlock), and one which Lucio is anxious to escape. In Act V scene 1 line 208 the Shakespeare coinage 'belocked' is used to denote the marriage contract.

Metal — a word much used in the play, associated imaginatively with prison and nunnery bars and chastity belts as well as the minting of coins. The homophone 'mettle' is also used punningly to introduce the idea of testing and valuing.

Grace — 'grace/gracious' is used three times in Act III scene 1 about Isabella. The word has religious significance as well as being a title denoting the Duke's rank, and is used by a variety of characters when addressing him. It is linked to the concepts of forgiveness and salvation. A moral of the play is that 'when once our grace we have forgot,/Nothing goes right' (IV.4.32).

Head — beheading is the form of execution in the play; maidenhead stands for virginity; the Duke is the head of state; a man is his wife's head (in two senses: her lord and her brains); and a head was stamped on coins. In Act IV scene 2 lines 3–5 the word is used in three of the senses. The phrase 'the head of Angelo' (IV.3.141) means yet another. One's head is the public and recognisable (or disguisable) part of the human body, and the one which represents the whole. The metaphor is actualised by the decapitated head of Ragozine.

Revelation — there are many cognate words related to the theme of deception: 'wrap', 'hidden', 'reveal', 'unfold', 'unmask'; nuns are not allowed to reveal their hair, or their faces if speaking. Mariana will not show her face until her husband bids her. The purpose of the final scene is to 'Unfold the evil which is here wrapped up' (line 117) and 'To make the truth appear where it seems hid' (line 66); this necessitates the revelations, physical and factual, of the Duke.

Meanings of the title

The actual title of *Measure for Measure* comes from the Sermon on the Mount reported in St Matthew's gospel (7:1–2):

> Judge not, that ye be not judged. For with what judgment ye judge, ye shall be judged: and with what measure ye mete, it shall be measured to you again.

However, it is quoted in the play ('Like doth quit like, and Measure still for Measure', V.1.408) with a different emphasis, and there are many other possible extensions of meaning of the title of the play. Consider the following:

- connected to the biblical concept that as one sows, so shall one reap (Galatians), and by extension to the belief that the end is contained in the beginning
- biblical parallel to 'an eye for an eye and a tooth for a tooth', i.e. the idea of Old Testament vengeance by the Lord
- moderation in all things, an Aristotelian prescription for a morally healthy life; 'a gentleman of all temperance' is how Escalus describes the Duke (III.2.227), whereas Lucio is 'a fellow of much licence' (III.2.195)
- appealing for a sense of balance to 'temper' the extremes and keep things in proportion, to avoid temptation

- step by step; one should take things gradually and carefully, along a line, applying reason with 'cold gradation and well-balanced form' (IV.3.98)
- Aristotle's definition of justice was that one should get what is proper for one, i.e. that the crime should match the punishment
- put yourself in the place of others, or 'do as you would be done by' (Matthew 7:12)
- tit-for-tat, or getting in first, deriving from a perversion of the above rule, often expressed as 'Do unto others as they would do unto you'; Angelo tries to pre-empt Isabella's public denunciation of him by accusing her of slander and madness
- a consistent response to the same action; it could be seen as anomalous that sexual congress is either condemned or blessed depending on the extremes dictated by the church, whereby the same act is viewed very differently according to whether it takes place in or out of wedlock
- Lord's prayer: 'Forgive us our trespasses that we may forgive them that trespass against us'
- as God treats man, so man treats his inferiors, passing justice down the line
- mutual concession is the only solution to antagonism; both sides must make a compromise to meet in the middle, as Isabella does
- justice cannot exist without some measure of injustice
- keep a balance in your life, i.e. between work and play, private and social
- don't overdo it and lose credibility; better to 'cut a little/Than fall, and bruise to death' (II.1.5–6)
- measure can mean sentence, as in 'He professes to have received no sinister measure from his judge' (III.2.232–33); the title can therefore refer to the judging and punishing of a crime
- a counteraction to negate an action, as in to take measures against something
- 'More nor less to others paying/Than by self-offences weighing' (III.2.253–54) is a recognition of your own sins in your treatment of others
- getting what you deserve, reward or punishment; Angelo first gets one and then the other
- the Provost says in IV.2.27–28 that human beings will be weighed for their crimes and will be found to be equally culpable
- a few lines later (IV.2.78–80), the Duke says that a judge must parallel his judgements with his own ability to practise 'holy abstinence'
- returning mercy and charity for pride and lust, humility for abuse of power, cancelling iniquity with justice
- 'her worth worth yours' (V.1.494); weighing humans to determine their relative moral stature
- 'What's mine is yours, and what is yours is mine' (V.1.534); marriage means that everything is equally shared

- when two things do not measure equally, for example if the man is not fit for the job, there is a bias or 'warp' (I.1.14)
- getting what you paid for; a system of measurement which makes trade in tavern and brothel possible
- we should treat everyone alike, even relatives on a par with strangers (II.2.81–82)
- we should treat heaven as we do ourselves (II.2.85–86)
- males and females should weigh and be treated equally, with rights, responsibilities and a voice
- Isabella weighs her brother's body against her own, and physical life against eternal life
- the Duke would, according to Lucio, have 'dark deeds darkly answered' (III.2.167), crimes punished secretly
- love should be a reciprocal experience of equal investment and return, getting out what you put in
- the day of judgement approaches like grains of sand dropping through an hour glass measuring time
- this play is the comic antidotal vision to *Othello*, as Shakespeare wrote one serious and one light play a year throughout his career, and these were both written in 1604
- contractual agreements, with clauses to benefit both parties
- the pendulum of human experience; 'for every action, there is an equal and opposite reaction' (Newton's third Law of Motion)
- those rising on the wheel of fortune are matched by those who are falling; and, ironically, 'Some rise by sin, and some by virtue fall' (II.1.38)
- good intention cancels evil deed: 'Might there not be a charity in sin/To save this brother's life?' (II.4.63–64)
- fighting evil with evil: 'Craft against vice I must apply' (III.2.265)

Quotations

The best quotations to know are those which you have found useful in class discussions and practice essays, and they will require little conscious learning because you are already familiar with them. The most effective ones to learn in addition are those which serve more than one purpose, i.e. which can be used to support a reference to theme or image usage as well as to make a point about character or dramatic effect.

Act I scene 1

- Let there be some more test made of my metal/Before so noble and so great a figure/Be stamped upon't. (Angelo to Duke)

Act I scene 2

- Thus can the demigod Authority/Make us pay down for our offence by weight/The words of heaven. On whom it will, it will;/On whom it will not, so: yet still 'tis just. (Claudio)
- So every scope by the immoderate use/Turns to restraint. (Claudio to Lucio)

Act I scene 3

- Believe not that the dribbling dart of love/Can pierce a complete bosom. (Duke)
- ...Lord Angelo,/A man of stricture and firm abstinence... (Duke)
- ...And liberty plucks justice by the nose;/The baby beats the nurse, and quite athwart/Goes all decorum. (Duke)
- Lord Angelo is precise,/Stands at a guard with envy, scarce confesses/That his blood flows... (Duke)
- Hence we shall see,/If power change purpose, what our seemers be. (Duke)

Act I scene 4

- I hold you as a thing enskied and sainted... (Lucio to Isabella)
- ...His givings-out were of an infinite distance/From his true-meant design. (Lucio about Duke)
- ...Lord Angelo, a man whose blood/Is very snow-broth... (Lucio)

Act II scene 1

- ...Let us be keen and rather cut a little/Than fall, and bruise to death. (Escalus to Angelo)
- 'Tis one thing to be tempted, Escalus,/Another thing to fall. (Angelo)
- ...Let mine own judgement pattern out my death/And nothing come in partial. (Angelo)
- Some rise by sin, and some by virtue fall... (Escalus)
- Which is the wiser here, Justice or Iniquity? (Escalus)
- Does your lordship mean to geld and splay all the youth of the city? (Pompey to Escalus)
- Lord Angelo is severe. (Justice)
- Mercy is not itself, that oft looks so;/Pardon is still the nurse of second woe. (Escalus)

Act II scene 2

- You are too cold. (Lucio to Isabella)
- O, 'tis excellent/To have a giant's strength, but it is tyrannous/To use it like a giant. (Isabella to Angelo)
- We cannot weigh our brother with ourself. (Isabella)
- She speaks, and 'tis/Such sense that my sense breeds with it. (Angelo)

- The tempter, or the tempted, who sins most? (Angelo)
- ...Thieves for their robbery have authority/When judges steal themselves. (Angelo)

Act II scene 4

- ...Let's write 'good Angel' on the devil's horn... (Angelo to himself)
- 'Tis set down so in heaven, but not in earth. (Isabella to Angelo)
- ...Might there not be a charity in sin/To save this brother's life? (Angelo to Isabella)
- Better it were a brother died at once/Than that a sister, by redeeming him,/Should die for ever. (Isabella)
- ...lawful mercy is/Nothing kin to foul redemption. (Isabella)
- We are all frail. (Angelo)
- I have begun/And now I give my sensual race the rein. (Angelo)
- ...my false o'erweighs your true. (Angelo to Isabella)
- Then, Isabel, live chaste, and, brother, die./More than our brother is our chastity. (Isabella)

Act III scene 1

- O, 'tis the cunning livery of hell,/The damnèd'st body to invest and cover/In precious guards. (Isabella to Claudio)
- Mercy to thee would prove itself a bawd,/'Tis best that thou diest quickly. (Isabella to Claudio)
- ...a marble to her tears (Duke to Isabella about Angelo's treatment of Mariana)

Act III scene 2

- That we were all, as some would seem to be,/Free from our faults, as faults from seeming free. (Duke)
- It was a mad fantastical trick of him to steal from the state... (Lucio to the disguised Duke about the Duke)
- A very superficial, ignorant, unweighing fellow. (Lucio to the disguised Duke about the Duke)
- The Duke yet would have dark deeds darkly answered. He would never bring them to light. (Lucio to the disguised Duke)
- ...back-wounding calumny/The whitest virtue strikes. What king so strong/Can tie the gall up in the slanderous tongue? (Duke to himself)
- That fellow is a fellow of much licence. (Escalus about Lucio)
- ...a gentleman of all temperance. (Escalus about the Duke)
- If his own life answer the straitness of his proceeding, it shall become him well; wherein if he chance to fail, he hath sentenced himself. (Duke to Escalus about Angelo)

- ...More nor less to others paying/Than by self-offences weighing. (Duke)
- O, what may man within him hide,/Though angel on the outward side? (Duke)
- Craft against vice I must apply. (Duke)

Act IV scene 1

- ...the justice of your title to him/Doth flourish the deceit. (Duke to Mariana about Angelo)

Act IV scene 2

- ...you weigh equally. A feather will turn the scale. (Provost to Abhorson about the professions of bawd and executioner)

Act IV scene 3

- I swear I will not die today for any man's persuasion. (Barnardine to Duke)
- O, 'tis an accident that heaven provides. (Duke)
- ...By cold gradation and well-balanced form,/We shall proceed with Angelo. (Duke to Provost)
- ...the old fantastical Duke of dark corners... (Lucio to disguised Duke)
- ...you'll answer this one day. (disguised Duke to Lucio)
- ...I am a kind of burr, I shall stick. (Lucio to disguised Duke)

Act IV scene 4

- Alack, when once our grace we had forgot,/Nothing goes right. We would, and we would not. (Angelo)

Act IV scene 6

- ...'tis a physic/That's bitter to sweet end. (Isabella to Mariana)

Act V scene 1

- ...justice, justice, justice, justice! (Isabella to Duke)
- ...for truth is truth/To th'end of reck'ning. (Isabella)
- ...let your reason serve/To make the truth appear where it seems hid... (Isabella to Duke)
- If he had so offended,/He would have weighed thy brother by himself,/And not have cut him off. (Duke to Isabella about Angelo)
- *Cucullus non facit monachum.* (Lucio)
- My business in this state/Made me a looker-on here in Vienna,/Where I have seen corruption boil and bubble/Till it o'errun the stew. (Duke as Lodowick)
- ...your grace, like power divine,/Hath looked upon my passes. (Angelo to Duke)
- 'An Angelo for Claudio, death for death!'/Haste still pays haste, and leisure answers leisure,/Like doth quit like, and Measure still for Measure. (Duke)

- They say best men are moulded out of faults... (Mariana)
- I partly think/A due sincerity governèd his deeds/Till he did look on me. (Isabella about Angelo)
- My brother had but justice,/In that he did the thing for which he died. (Isabella)
- ...I crave death more willingly than mercy. (Angelo)
- I find an apt remission in myself,/And yet here's one in place I cannot pardon. (Duke about Lucio)
- Th'offence pardons itself. (Duke)

Literary terms and concepts

The terms and concepts below have been selected for their relevance to talking and writing about *Measure for Measure*. It will aid argument and expression to become familiar with them and to use them in your discussions and essays.

advocatus diaboli literally the devil's lawyer, this usually means arguing a case one does not actually believe, or representing the wrong side

allegory extended metaphor which veils a moral or political underlying meaning

ambiguity capacity of words to have two simultaneous meanings in the same context, either accidentally or, more often, as a deliberate device for enriching the meaning of text

ambivalence simultaneous coexistence of opposing feelings or attitudes

anacoluthon syntactical breakdown whereby what follows is ungrammatical

antithesis contrast of ideas expressed by balancing words or phrases of opposite meaning

Apollonian of or relating to Apollo, god of light, poetry, music, healing and prophecy

aside remark spoken by a character in a play which is shared with the audience but unheard by some or all of the other characters on stage

black comedy treating serious or painful subjects, e.g. death, as amusing

blank verse unrhymed **iambic pentameter**, the staple form of Shakespeare's plays

Bowdler(ise) Thomas Bowdler in 1818 published a 10-volume edition of

Shakespeare's works from which he had removed all the improper words; to censor sexual references

caesura deliberate break or pause in a line of verse, signified by punctuation

choric like a chorus in a Greek drama whose role was to comment on the action and interpret its moral significance

climax moment of intensity to which a series of actions has been leading

colloquial informal language of speech rather than that of writing

comedy Ancient Greek form of drama in which confusions and deceptions are unravelled, with amusement along the way, ending in resolution, restitution and reconciliation

crux (pl cruces) point of disagreement between critics about words of a text

dénouement unfolding of the final stages of a plot, when all is revealed

deus ex machina literally, the god from the machine; it refers to a supernatural intervention which resolves a difficult situation

Dionysiac of or relating to Dionysus, Greek god of wine, fruitfulness and vegetation, and worshipped in orgiastic rites

dramatic irony when the audience knows something the character speaking does not

enjambement run-on line of verse, usually to reflect its meaning

hubris over-reaching of a human who, from pride or presumption, aspires to divine power or status, resulting in downfall, which is the punishment by Nemesis, the goddess of retribution

iambic pentameter five feet of iambs, i.e. alternating unstressed/stressed syllables; tetrameter has four feet and hexameter (alexandrines) has six

imagery figurative descriptive language; a pattern of related images that helps to build up mood and atmosphere, and develop the themes of a literary work

in medias res beginning a scene or chapter in the middle of an event or dialogue

irony a discrepancy between the actual and implied meaning of

	language; or an amusing or cruel reversal of an outcome expected, intended or deserved; situation in which one is mocked by fate or the facts
Machiavellian	early sixteenth-century political philosophy proposed by the Italian Niccolo Machiavelli in the book *The Prince*, which recommended ruthless self-interest and unethical methods to gain political power
malapropism	ludicrous misuse of a word in mistake for one resembling it, as in Elbow's 'two notorious benefactors' (II.1.49) and 'detest before heaven' (II.1.66)
neologism	creation of a new word, e.g. 'circummured' (IV.1.27)
oxymoron	phrase consisting of a contradiction in terms, e.g. 'devilish mercy' (III.1.68)
paradox	self-contradictory statement or state of affairs
pathos	pity evoked by a situation of suffering and helplessness, e.g. Mariana's situation
pun	use of a word with double meaning for humorous or ironic effect
Rabelaisian	obsessed with sexual acts, bodily functions and ribaldry in the mode of the early sixteenth-century French writer, Rabelais
rhyming couplet	a pair of adjacent rhyming lines
seven deadly sins	according to the medieval Catholic church, the following sins were mortal and led straight to Hell: pride, envy, gluttony, lechery, avarice, wrath, sloth; many contemporary and later literary works include these sins symbolically or thematically
soliloquy	speech given by a character alone on stage which reveals their thoughts
symbol	object, person or event which represents something more than itself, e.g. the sounding of a trumpet symbolises the Day of Judgement
theme	abstract idea or issue explored in a literary work, distinct from the content

tragedy   Ancient Greek form of drama or other literary work of a serious nature traditionally concerning men in high positions, with a fatal conclusion for the guilty and the innocent; characterised by waste, loss and a fall from power

verse   language organised according to its rhythmical qualities into regular patterns of metre and set out in lines

Questions & Answers

Essay questions, specimen plans and notes

Essay questions

The example essay questions which follow can be used for planning practice and full essay writing within the time limit, with or without the text. Many have been previously set by different exam boards for various specifications. Remember to talk about the play and the audience, not the book and the reader, and try to visualise how it would appear on stage and how it would sound; the drama and the poetry are essential elements of the written text you are being asked to respond to. Remember, also, that themes are relevant to all essays, and that analysis, not just description, is always required. Exam essays should be clearly structured, briskly argued, concisely expressed, closely focused, and supported by brief but constant textual references. They should show a combination of familiarity, understanding, analytical skill and informed personal response. Length is not in itself an issue — quality matters rather than quantity — but you have to prove your knowledge and fulfil the assessment criteria, and without sufficient coverage and exploration of the title you cannot be awarded a top mark. Aim realistically for approximately 12 paragraphs or four sides of A4.

Whole-text questions: closed text

1 'It is essential to the development of the play's tragic situation that the Duke, Angelo and Isabella are committed Christians.' How far do you agree with this view? In your answer you should discuss characters and motives, narrative development and setting. You should also show an awareness of Elizabethan attitudes to gender and sexual morality.

2 'It is unconvincing that Isabella should agree to marry the Duke.' Do you think that there is any evidence for this view?

3 How do you see the relationship between church and state? What is its importance in the play?

4 Claudio and Lucio are companions and friends, yet they are different in character. Explore the differences between them. With which of them do your sympathies lie when you see or read the play?

5 'What king so strong/Can tie the gall up in the slanderous tongue?' What exactly is being said here, and how does it relate to the play as a whole?

6 'Desire in the play is not confined to Angelo.' Where else is it important?

7 Describe and interpret the roles of the women in *Measure for Measure*.

8 'Men are the sport of circumstances when/Circumstances seem the sport of men'

(Lord Byron). How far is it true that Angelo becomes trapped by his own deviousness?

9 'Might there not be a charity in sin/To save this brother's life?' Explore the idea of charity in *Measure for Measure*.

10 The play's problem is Shakespeare's 'failure to make Isabella a consistent character'. Do you agree?

11 'The enduring interest of the play is its treatment of sexual politics.' Do you agree?

12 How does Shakespeare convey the strengths and weaknesses of Duke Vincentio's character?

13 'In *Measure for Measure* Shakespeare explores the nature of class prejudice.' How far does your reading of the play support this view?

14 *Measure for Measure* is clearly a comedy since it teaches all the characters to be 'sensible of mortality'. Explore this comment.

15 Do you agree that the quality of the play deteriorates about halfway through? Support your opinion using arguments which refer to the play as both text and performance.

16 Angelo and Lucio's punishment of forced marriage is as immoral as their crimes against the women they exploited. Do you agree?

17 How successful is Shakespeare in creating a decadent environment and a licentious atmosphere in *Measure for Measure*, and to what dramatic use does he put them?

18 'The main theme of *Measure for Measure* is marriage.' Explore this claim.

19 Is the comedy integral to the plot of *Measure for Measure*, or does it distract and detract from it?

20 *Measure for Measure* has no relevance to the modern age of sexual freedom and liberal laws. Do you agree?

21 'The action of *Measure for Measure* is no less than the Fall of Man, the failure of humanity.' Examine and evaluate this proposition.

22 As a director, how would you wish to present Angelo or Isabella in a production of the play? In the course of your answer:
- explain clearly those aspects of his or her character that you would want to emphasise
- comment on what the play suggests about Shakespeare's presentation of good and evil

23 *Measure for Measure* had a history of unpopularity with critics and audiences until the twentieth century, when its reputation rose considerably in both respects. Why do you think this should be?

24 'We are all frail', as Angelo says. Is it fair to say that *Measure for Measure* concerns itself with defining the qualities and limitations of humanity?

25 '*Measure for Measure* is a play which exposes the futility of rigid, systematised

judgements of human conduct.' Discuss your own view of judgement as portrayed in this play.

26 Do you agree that it is the women in *Measure for Measure* who symbolise the iniquity of society, and who also redeem it?

27 'For truth is truth/To th'end of reck'ning.' Comment on Isabella's statement in the context of the play.

28 '*Measure for Measure* not only blurs the distinctions between good and evil, but suggests that they can be interchangeable.' Discuss.

29 Coleridge described *Measure for Measure* as 'a hateful work'. What do you think he meant, and do you agree with his opinion?

30 'A feather will turn the scale.' Discuss the implications of this quotation for the play as a whole.

31 *Measure for Measure* has been described as 'this terrible encounter of absolutes'. Discuss the meaning and appropriateness of this description.

32 Discuss the role of vows, oaths and promises in *Measure for Measure*.

33 'We learn along with the Duke, by seeing all the action from his point of view.' Is this a satisfactory explanation of the role of the Duke?

34 *Measure for Measure* fully explores the ambivalent attitude of society towards human sexuality. Do you agree?

35 'Shakespeare's fault lies in giving Isabella no transitions.' Do you agree that this is why it is difficult for an audience to sympathise with Isabella?

36 How does Shakespeare convey that Vienna represents a world of 'tottering values and disordered will', and what is the significance of this portrayal?

37 Everyone in the play is either a doubter or a seemer, except Barnardine. Is this a true assessment of the characters of *Measure for Measure*?

38 'That it presents problems to which there are no final solutions, either in the play or outside of it, is a measure of its success, not its failure.' Do you agree with this verdict on *Measure for Measure*?

39 To what extent do you think that Isabella is a failure, dramatically speaking?

40 The Duke's philosophy is one of 'cold gradation and well-balanced form'. What do you understand by this phrase, and how does it apply to the Duke and the play as a whole?

41 *Measure for Measure* is about 'ponderous and substantial things'. What are they?

42 Pater said that Shakespeare 'conveys to us a strong sense of the tyranny of nature and circumstance over human action'. Is this your interpretation of the play?

43 G. B. Shaw said that one always feels when one has learnt something that one has lost something. How would you apply this view to *Measure for Measure*?

44 Who has learned what in the course of *Measure for Measure*?

45 Does the final solution answer the questions raised in *Measure for Measure*?

46 'To err is human, to forgive divine' (Pope). How can this be applied to *Measure for Measure*?

47 Do you agree that *Measure for Measure* is essentially a play of forgiveness?

48 'In *Measure for Measure*, justice itself is on trial.' Do you agree that this is the focus of the play, and if so, what is the verdict?

49 How do the men's views on women and female sexuality cause the action of the play?

50 'The problem with *Measure for Measure* is that there are no characters for whom an audience may have sympathy.' To what extent do you agree with this comment?

51   O, what may man within him hide,
    Though angel on the outward side?

    Craft against vice I must apply.

Both these quotations come from Vincentio's soliloquy at the end of Act III. Using them as a starting point, write about the significance of deception and disguise in *Measure for Measure*.

52 'The play is about judgement, but Shakespeare never judges.' Do you feel this is true as applied to *Measure for Measure*?

Specimen plans and notes

Below are ten past essay titles set by different exam boards, each followed by either examiner notes or a possible plan.

1 Explore the links that Shakespeare presents between self-knowledge and virtue in two of the following characters from *Measure for Measure*.
  - Angelo
  - Claudio
  - Isabella

Self-knowledge and virtue – human values thrown into relief/tested; characters forced to reassess their concepts of what constitutes virtue; tensions between lechery and right conduct; good sense and reason overcoming passion leading to virtuous conduct, with humanist/Christian notions of charity and kindness set against 'pagan' notions of shame and sin; Isabella's 'virtue' reliant initially on spiritual absolutes; secular and divine justice. Play parallels breakdown of integrity and social order; justice finally 'assayed'.
(Source: Examiner notes, AQA B, January 2002)

2 To what extent do the marriages arranged at the end of the play between Lucio and Kate Keepdown, Angelo and Mariana, and Claudio and Juliet bring to a satisfactory conclusion the social and moral issues raised earlier in the play?
Concept of comic harmony – expected to result in marriage but – how far are social/moral issues resolved in relation to the three marriages cited? What kind of conduct is socially acceptable? Natural honesty and charity set against notions of vulgarity/handfast marriage

acceptability (since oral vows made between A. and M.). Are moral values subverted by the genre's need for final harmony?

(Source: Examiner notes, AQA B, January 2002)

3 **Discuss the reasons why *Measure for Measure* might be termed 'a problem play'.**
Candidates do not need any detailed knowledge of other plays in order to answer this question effectively. The context of genre is important in this question: indeed, there is a 'problem' in assigning this play to any particular genre. The term 'problem play' has been imposed by readers, but the history of critical responses to the play justifies this. We can expect much discussion of the ending which superficially follows the conventions of comedy, while being full of moral and arguably dramatic ambivalence.

(Source: Examiner notes, AQA B, June 2002)

4 **Compare and contrast the ideas of justice held by Escalus and by Angelo.**
The content highlighted here is the concept of justice; held by two contrasting characters in relation, perhaps, to the idea of justice propounded within the play as a whole. Obviously the focus of answers must be on Escalus and Angelo, but more sophisticated responses will be aware of the importance of other conceptions of justice held by other characters.

(Source: Examiner notes, AQA B, June 2002)

5 **Isabella defines Angelo as an 'arch-villain'. To what extent do you agree with her that Angelo is the villain of the play?**
The quotation from the play defines Angelo as an 'arch-villain', yet the question only asks candidates to discuss whether Angelo is a 'villain'. Better answers may well note the subtle difference but this is not essential to achieving high marks. Candidates may offer their definition of a villain as a starting point for discussion and we should accept any reasonable offering. Straightforward character descriptions of Angelo would not particularly address contextual issues, and answers should evaluate Angelo's actions against the moral and/or literary or theatrical context of 'villainy'. Some sense of the political and moral values presented in the play will be inherent in a good answer. Examiners should be prepared for a range of differing responses to Angelo's character. Some candidates may be sympathetic to Angelo's unsolicited position of responsibility and his inexperience; others may condemn his lack of self-knowledge and hypocrisy.

(Source: Examiner notes, AQA B, January 2003)

6 **Do you consider that the events in Act V make a fitting end to the play as a whole?**
This question requires candidates to see Act V in relation to the play as a whole and consider its dramatic and literary context. Some awareness of an audience's expectations for the final act of a play would be worthy of credit, and discussion of how those expectations relate to genre, together with the problems of assigning this particular play to a definite genre may make a good answer. Mere plot summaries are unlikely to score highly but try to be alert to the type of answer where some commentary is intermingled with or inherent in plot summary. Candidates may consider the significance of the Duke's 'return'

and how he orchestrates it; the final revelations and issues of forgiveness and union, particularly marriage. The question does ask candidates to evaluate how 'fitting' these events are, so some indication of personal response is required.

(Source: Examiner notes, AQA B, January 2003)

7 **To what extent do you consider the Duke, Vincentio, to be an irresponsible ruler?**

Focus: an assessment of Vincentio's role in the play with particular reference to his role as a head of state.

Possible content: AO5 is addressed by inviting candidates to consider Vincentio's role as a ruler. Social and political context must be involved in any assessment of Vincentio's responsibility as a ruler. Many candidates may see his actions as a denial and abnegation of his duties and be critical of him. Others may be more sympathetic and seek valid reasons within the text for his actions. Cogent argument of either viewpoint should be rewarded.

(Source: Examiner notes, AQA B, June 2003)

8   More than our brother is our chastity. (Isabella)

What sin you do to save a brother's life,
Nature dispenses with the deed so far
That it becomes a virtue. (Claudio)

How far do you see the moral issues presented by these two quotations as central to the play as a whole?

Focus: a consideration of the central moral issues at stake, evaluating whether chastity or life itself is of greater value.

Possible content: candidates in the past have shown an obvious desire to engage with these issues so this question should give them that opportunity! Some may be very severe on Isabella's refusal to give up her virtue for her brother's life but others may show a greater contextual awareness of the theological consequences of sin (AO5). Better answers will explore the complexities of the situation and not see it in simple terms of black and white. The question also invites some assessment of these issues within the context of the play as a whole and whether the moral issues are of central importance. Well-substantiated literary arguments should be rewarded.

(Source: Examiner notes, AQA B, June 2003)

9 **What are Angelo's views on women and female sexuality, and how do they relate to those typical of the period?**

Possible ideas to include in a plan

- medieval and Elizabethan church regarded women as dangerous to men's souls because of the seduction of Adam by Eve and the Fall of Man
- women's chastity was crucial, as illegitimacy was seen as threat to social and legal fabric
- the only sexually available, unchaperoned women were prostitutes, or considered to be so

- lust, one of the seven deadly sins, was a besetting sin for men of the period, and a particular problem for those who aimed for religious office, since celibacy was a requirement
- Angelo's view is typical in that he distrusts and fears women, yet is tempted by and attracted to them
- marriage was a matter of contract and agreement between the men involved, based on assumed virginity of woman; the father or brother had to provide the dowry; Angelo destroys Mariana's reputation because of disappointment in expectation of money, and she must therefore withdraw from society as she has no acceptable social role, being unmanned
- Angelo is susceptible to Isabella's beauty and speech, and cannot resist the temptation she represents, though he knows he will be damned for it
- he sees her as a kind of devil as well as an innocent nun, a paradox typical of the male attitude to women over the centuries; they are allocated two possible extreme roles of virgin/angel and whore/demon
- he denies women a 'tongue' and autonomous behaviour; he assumes Isabella and Mariana are following male orders in denouncing him (which they are)
- his forced marriage to Mariana, in order to save her reputation, is not greeted enthusiastically (he would rather die) and is on a par with that of Lucio to Kate Keepdown
- he sees women as inferior and does not accept that he owes Mariana or Isabella anything; his sphere of interest is entirely male and to do with his relationship with himself, with God, and with the Duke, spiritual and temporal power being the exclusive prerogative of men; women belong to the private not the public domain

10 '*Measure for Measure* is concerned with error, not with evil.' Discuss the differences between the two, and say whether you agree with this description of the play.

Possible ideas to include in a plan
- tragedy deals with evil, but comedy deals with error
- if the action of *Measure for Measure* is no less than the Fall of Man, the failure of humanity, then it concerns evil
- Satan was evil, and allowed in through Adam and Eve's error, therefore error of judgement is an entrance for evil and one leads to the other, as failure to uphold the law (error) breeds evil actions and crimes, including murder (Barnardine)
- all humans are by definition fallen and imperfect, and therefore prone to error
- the state deals with error and the church with evil, but the Duke personifies both
- error is unintentional and caused by misjudgement; giving way to temptation and breaking of oaths is done deliberately in full knowledge of the consequences of the choice, to oneself and others, and is therefore evil (Angelo and Lucio v. Claudio, who 'was ever precise in promise-keeping')
- 'a feather will turn the scale' between error and evil?

- the potential destructiveness of evil is averted only by divine intervention; the *deus ex machina* of the Duke
- the play focuses on correction of, not retribution for, previous errors; this is clear in Act V; no evils are actually committed, only intended
- 'to err is human, to forgive divine'; this clarifies the Duke's role as judge
- recognition of error and acceptance of sentence, including mercy, form the test of true repentance; does Angelo pass the test?
- it is an error in humans to think they can be superhumanly good; Angelo and Isabella share this hubris; also an error to be immoderate and intolerant
- 'slanderous tongues' (deliberately, not accidentally causing harm) are treated as the greatest evil in the play, hence the Duke's attitude to Lucio; Angelo has let loose slanderous tongues against Mariana and also slanders Isabella in Act V, calling her mad
- it is an error not to be 'sensible of mortality', i.e. not to prepare for inevitable death by being in a state of grace and asking forgiveness for sins

Sample essays

Below are two sample essays written by different students. Both of them have been assessed as falling within the top band. You can judge them against the Assessment Objectives for this text for your exam board and decide on the mark you think each deserves and why. You will also be able to see ways in which each could be improved in terms of content, style and accuracy.

Sample essay 1

In what sense may *Measure for Measure* be justly termed a dark comedy?

Measure for Measure, the last of Shakespeare's great comedies, is also the darkest of his comedies, and represents his transition to tragic plays. This play differs from Shakespeare's other comedies, and is in many ways more akin to tragedy than to comedy. In setting, plot, and character *Measure for Measure* has a tragic tone, and even the comic characters, e.g. Lucio the slanderer and Abhorson the executioner, are sinister. The language of the play is also dark, with many references to death and places deprived of light. However, because none of the main characters actually loses his life, this play is considered a comedy.

Almost all of Shakespeare's comedies have dual localities: the real world of crime, punishment, and responsibility, and an idyllic world, where reality is malleable, and forgiving. For example, *As You Like It* occurs in both the world of the court, dangerous for almost all of the primary characters, and the forest of Arden, a sanctuary that nurses conflict to resolution. *Measure for Measure*, on the other hand, offers no safe haven for the characters. They are trapped in the corrupted mire called Vienna. Angelo, appointed scourge of the city, lets no person escape his punishing hand. The play focuses on the gravity of the situation with little emotional respite for the audience and characters. Time is running out for Claudio and the Duke, and vice is becoming more not less powerful, and it is difficult to be sure that evil will be punished, especially after Barnardine's refusal to accept his sentence, and after Lucio has brought into doubt the integrity of the Duke.

Measure for Measure is dangerously close to being a tragedy throughout the whole play. Claudio's death seems imminent; Isabella will lose either her brother by preserving her chastity, or lose her future as a nun by sacrificing her virginity to the misnamed Angelo; and Angelo, whose hyper-moral reign of terror has no sway over his own actions, nearly perverts the entire plot to his own lust. Many difficult philosophical questions are raised but left unanswered by the play, such as 'The tempter, or the tempted, who sins most?' and 'Mercy is not itself, that oft looks so; Pardon is still the nurse of second woe'. Cynical comments are made and are allowed to go unchallenged even about the validity of justice: 'On whom it will, it will; On whom it will not, so: yet still 'tis just' and 'Thieves for their robbery have authority/When judges steal themselves' are statements which undermine the authority of the Duke as judge and sound more like the utterances of characters in a tragedy such as *King Lear*.

The characters are 'absolutists', as Anne Barton wrote in an introduction to the play, and therefore rigidly and stubbornly stick by their beliefs and refuse to compromise, thereby working against the spirit of comedy and inviting tragedy, as what cannot bend must break. Angelo's extreme character and ruthless scheming are similar to that of Iago in *Othello*. Only the Duke's manipulation enables a disastrous outcome to be avoided, and there are questions about his real motive in the play in any case. Is his pretended absence just a trick to catch the 'seemer' who betrayed Mariana, or does he really believe Vienna needs 'A man of stricture and firm abstinence' to apply the laws, as there certainly seems need of someone to do the job properly? It is by no means certain that characters have learned to mend their ways in the play – Lucio, Pompey, Froth, and Angelo for instance – although the process of comedy is supposed to make everyone wiser. The foolery of the so-called comic element, itself concerning disease and execution, cannot lift the weight of seriousness of the issues of the play.

The entire play bears a tragic weight that Shakespeare lifts only in the final moments and the 'happy' ending clashes with the previous events. The Duke, sometimes sinister mastermind of the plot, forces the final judgement on the characters, and offers little real relief. For example, the Duke demands that Isabella, who seemed set on a chaste life as a nun, marry him. The plot has thrown her from one precarious situation to another, and she is finally left with no real option but to marry the Duke. Shakespeare provides no evidence that Isabella wants this, nor does he allow her any real escape from the Duke's demand. In essence, she is in the same position with the Duke as she was with Angelo. The Duke cruelly pretends that Claudio, Isabella's beloved brother is dead; he pretends to side with Angelo, thereby exacerbating the mental anguish of Mariana and Isabella; he bolsters Angelo's confidence that he will escape punishment. Though no one dies, except Ragozine, several of the characters might prefer death to the sentence the Duke hands out, using marriage more as a punishment than a reward, unlike in the other comedies. The title of the play comes from the Bible and the play has a heavy feeling of death and day of judgement hanging over it which it never manages to escape.

Sample essay 2

How does Shakespeare convey the strengths and weaknesses of Duke Vincentio's character in *Measure for Measure*?

As Leavis said 'ultimately what one makes of the ending […] depends on what one makes of the Duke' and many critics and viewers find him anything from baffling to criminal in his behaviour. Though his symbolic Christian role is clear, as a dispenser of divine mercy and retribution in the Day of Judgement in Act V, his actual role seems more ambiguous, partly because he is also in disguise as Friar Lodowick and partly because his attitude to Angelo at the beginning of the play is contradictory. There is also a problem inherent in the fact that the Duke is required to be both a 'looker-on' who has to learn the truth about his subjects and his fellow judges and quickly respond, and the all-knowing magistrate who has planned everything in advance and is fully in control of the proceedings. He also has to play the role of someone immune to 'the dribbling dart of love' and yet be a worthy future husband for Isabella.

The Duke has the strength of his spiritual and political status as divinely appointed ruler with 'demigod Authority'. He is omniscient and ultimately omnipotent, as we can see from his overruling of Angelo and the imposition of his own wishes and decrees on everyone in the final trial scene. By keeping his emotions checked and following the rules of the wise magistrate – 'By cold gradation and well-balanced form,/We shall proceed with Angelo' – he is able to show himself to be above ordinary mortals and worthy of his rank. Even Angelo concedes his 'grace, like power divine'. The 'Duke of dark corners' knows everything which is happening in Vienna, and was arguably fully aware of the real Angelo behind the 'seemer' from the beginning.

However, by renouncing his rule at the beginning, this is a show of weakness which would have alarmed contemporary audiences, who had precedents historical and literary for the disasters which befell leaderless states or usurped thrones. Shakespeare deals with the same issue again in his final play, *The Tempest*, which also has a ruler of an Italian state who does not concentrate on his duty as ruler but is more interested in his books. The prince was thought to be God's representative on earth and judge of his fellow men, and it is a serious weakness to which the Duke admits when he says that the laws of Vienna have not been implemented for 14 (or 19) years. It is a further weakness if he has been fooled by appearances and believes that his 'precise' deputy will make a good judge.

It is also a sign of humanity, and therefore fallibility, that the Duke is not fully in control of Claudio's fate, given that Angelo breaks his word to release him, or of the timings of events. He is nearly caught out by the fact that the Provost is ordered to bring forward Claudio's execution and but for the chance – 'an accident that heaven provides' – that

Ragozine is available to have his head substituted, the Duke's plan would go awry. That the Duke cannot persuade Barnardine to submit to die according to the law of Vienna is also a clear indication of the limits of the Duke's powers. Without craft to apply against vice, he would be powerless to root out the evil growing and spreading through the streets, bawdy houses and palaces of Vienna. He has to stoop to eavesdropping, disguise and the 'dark deeds' of the enemy. Furthermore, he cannot resist Isabella's charms and preserve his bachelorhood, and there is also the strong suggestion that he is unable to curb Lucio's slanderous tongue, even at the very end of the play.

That the Duke has both strengths and weaknesses creates the comedy outcome of the play, whereby he can order everything in Act V and dispense rewards and punishments in divine fashion, but also remind the audience of the limitations of humanity (as Angelo says, 'We are all frail'), and that even the highest and noblest are subject themselves to a higher authority, and to time and chance, and must themselves be judged and taught lessons. In this he is similar to Prospero in *The Tempest*. Though he has supreme temporal power, he is fundamentally a man who has made mistakes and given in to temptations, and these weaknesses have made him stronger and wiser. It is this human side, rather than his role as providence, which makes him interesting in a way in which the dukes of earlier comedies, who are only symbols or plot devices, are not. It may be relevant to remember that many critics see Duke Vincentio as representing England's new monarch, James I, who was thought to possess intellectual and political skills but also to have a tendency to seek seclusion and to indulge whimsicality where the law was concerned – a mixture of strengths and weaknesses.

Further study

Editions

Gibson, R. (ed.) (1993) *Cambridge School Shakespeare*, Cambridge University Press.
Lever, J. W. (ed.) (1965) *The Arden Shakespeare*, Methuen/Nelson.
Nosworthy, J. M. (ed.) (1969) *New Penguin Shakespeare*, Penguin.
Quiller-Couch, A. and Wilson, J. D. (eds) (1969) *The New Shakespeare*, Cambridge University Press.

Critical works

Bate, J. (1998) *The Genius of Shakespeare*, Picador.
Clemen, W. (1951) *The Development of Shakespeare's Imagery*, Harvard University Press.
Empson, W. (1995) *Seven Types of Ambiguity*, Penguin.
Empson, W. (1995) *The Structure of Complex Words*, Penguin.
Hawkes, T. (ed.) (1969) *Coleridge on Shakespeare*, Penguin Shakespeare Library.

Honigmann, E. A. J. (1989) *Myriad-Minded Shakespeare*, Macmillan.

Kermode, F. (2001) *Shakespeare's Language*, Penguin.

Knight, G. Wilson (2001) *The Wheel of Fire*, Routledge.

Lawrence, W. W. (1969) *Shakespeare's Problem Comedies*, Penguin Shakespeare Library.

Mahood, M. M. (1968) *Shakespeare's Wordplay*, Methuen.

Muir, K. (ed.) (1965) *Shakespeare, the Comedies (Twentieth Century Views)*, Prentice Hall.

Neely, C. T. (1985) *Broken Nuptials in Shakespeare Plays*, University of Illinois Press.

Palmer, D. J. (1971) *Shakespeare's Later Comedies*, Penguin Shakespeare Library.

Rossiter, A. P. (1989) *Angel with Horns: 15 Lectures on Shakespeare*, Longman.

Spurgeon, C. F. E. (1935) *Shakespeare's Imagery and What It Tells Us*, Cambridge University Press.

Stead, C. K. (1971) *Shakespeare's Measure for Measure (Casebook series)*, Macmillan.

Stone, L. (1990) *The Family, Sex and Marriage in England 1500–1800*, Penguin.

Tillyard, E. M. W. (1970) *Shakespeare's Problem Plays*, Penguin.

Films

No commercial film has ever been made.

1979: BBC Shakespeare, with Tim Piggott Smith.

1994: BBC2 version, with Tom Wilkinson.

Internet

There are now a vast number of sites on the internet with useful material on Shakespeare and *Measure for Measure*. A Google search for 'Measure for Measure' returns 221,000 pages. A word of warning: the internet is a highly volatile place, and sites come and go with bewildering rapidity. Links lists become out of date very quickly, but if you try a site and are disappointed by an 'Error 404 — Not Found' message, move on; there will be many more sites, and the quality is generally improving with the passing of time. There is also a tendency to charge for content which was once free. It is hard to judge before parting with money, but often similar material can be found free if you are patient and thorough in your use of search engines.

- **http://shakespeare.palomar.edu/** *Mr William Shakespeare and the Internet* is one of the best general Shakespeare sites. It includes general information and an extensive set of links to other sites, many of which include the full text of some or all of the plays, listed at **http://shakespeare.palomar.edu/works.htm.** Most of these have some form of search engine which allows the text to be searched for words or phrases.

- **www.eamesharlan.org/tptt/** This site includes a word count, and line-count by character, for each play.

In addition to relevant sections on *Measure for Measure* in or referred to in the sites above, there are a number of individual sites worthy of note:

- **www.sparknotes.com/shakespeare/measure/** is a good introductory site, with the full text, notes and search engine
- **www.online-literature.com/shakespeare/measure/** has text and scene summaries
- **http://web.uvic.ca/shakespeare/Annex/DraftTxt/MM/index.html** gives the play, accessible by scene or by page
- **www.shakespeares-globe.org/** is the official website of the reconstructed Globe Theatre
- **www.shakespeare.org.uk** is the site of the Shakespeare Birthplace Trust

Individual essays on *Measure for Measure*, of varying quality, include:

- **www.marshall.edu/engsr/SR1996.html#Wishing** 'Wishing a more strict restraint': feminist performance and the silence of Isabella'
- **www.marshall.edu/engsr/SR1996.html#Redemption** 'Redemption and damnation: *Measure for Measure* and *Othello* as contrasting paired visions'
- **www.shakespeare-online.com/essays/measureessays.html** also provides a good collection of essays, but not all of the links work